PEPPERS

HOT & SWEET

PEPPERS
HOT & SWEET

Beth Dooley

A Garden Way Publishing Book

Storey Communications, Inc.
Schoolhouse Road
Pownal, Vermont 05261

I dedicate this book to Kevin, Matt, and Kip

Front cover photograph by David J. Bausman
Cover Stylist Beth Dooley
Cover & Text designed and produced by Nancy Lamb
Edited by Constance L. Oxley

The name Garden Way Publishing is licensed to Storey Communications, Inc.
by Garden Way, Inc.

Printed in the United States by Courier
First Printing, August 1990

Library of Congress Catalog Card Number: 90-55044
International Standard Book Number: 0-88266-622-3 (pbk.)
                                    0-88266-621-5 (hc)
Library of Congress Cataloging-in-Publication Data
Dooley, Beth
         Peppers, hot and sweet : over 100 recipes for all tastes / by Beth Dooley.
                  p.   cm.
         "A Garden Way Publishing book."
         Includes index.
         ISBN 0-88266-622-3 — ISBN 0-88266-621-5 (pbk.)
         1. Cookery (Peppers)   I. Title.
         TX803.P46D66   1990
         641.6'5643—dc20   90-55044
                              CIP

ACKNOWLEDGMENT

The author would especially like to thank Ann Burckhardt for her long hours of proofing the manuscript and for her friendship and support.

CONTENTS

THE VERY WORD "PEPPER" tickles the tongue — perking fiery flavors and exotic tastes in a palette of crisp colors. It conjures up images of exotic foods from foreign lands, Mexico, China, Africa, India, the Caribbean. When I think of peppers, I long for summertime when the living is easy and the food so very fresh.

Here, the Minneapolis Farmer's Market is a garden of earthly delights. Early mornings through the summer, local growers share their harvest of corn, tomatoes, and glossy red, yellow, and green bell peppers. The Hmong women merchants pile their stands with tiny red and green chiles, plump cherry peppers, and heaps of cilantro. In willing but broken English, they give cooking tips for peppers in a stir-fry or spicy dip.

Each stall reflects the colorful enthusiasm of its owner, recalling the vegetable stands I shopped at with my grandmother as a child. I'd tag along on her biweekly expeditions to the New Jersey countryside near her summer home on the Shore. She took her time sniffing tomatoes, thumping melons, and holding each green or red bell pepper up to the light to examine for soft spots. Often she'd stop to chat about the farmer's crops, the weather, or to swap a new recipe, clipped from the local paper and tagged to her shopping list.

My grandmother's food was fresh and colorful. After a day on the beach, to our sun-ripened appetites, nothing ever tasted so good. She brightened up succotash with strips of red bell pepper and tossed chopped red and green bells into "confetti" slaw. She fried sweet Italian peppers with onions and baked them stuffed with meat loaf. When we sat at her dining room table, in the evening glow of fatigue, listening to the hum of our parents' conversation, no one ever had to say, "eat your vegetables."

WITHOUT REWRITING HISTORY, it's safe to say that Christopher Columbus' great discovery was the result of misdirected efforts. He set sail from Spain in search of a quicker route to the East Indies. Here, friendly natives welcomed the crew with a colorful, piquant cuisine, made with the sweet and spicy fruits Columbus named "peppers." He carried pepper seeds back to Spain where they quickly adapted to Old World soil and peppers were adopted into Old World cuisine. Besides expanding the Western horizon, Columbus opened the world to capsicum peppers: mild and sweet, green, yellow, orange, red, and purple bells, and spicy hot and fiery chiles.

There is no botanical relationship between the *piper nigrum* plant that produces black, white, or green peppercorns and the many varieties of the *Capsicum* genus or bell and chile peppers. Our English language creates terrific confusion by calling both by the same name. Other languages have identified them differently. The French, for example, call for *piment* when they want hot pepper to spice up an omelette or *poivre* to grind over tossed salad.

Pepper seeds were carried from the royal Spanish gardens to Africa, India, and Asia by sixteenth century traders. It's ironic that chile and bell peppers have become an important ingredient in the cuisines of countries that produce peppercorns. Who can imagine an Indian curry, Szechwan stir-fry, or African peanut sauce without the fiery kick?

South American countries have used peppers for millennia. Archaeological evidence suggests that natives of Peru and Brazil began eating bell and chile peppers as early as 6500 B.C. The Aztecs and Incas share credit for many of the varieties we know today. In Mexico, the chile was revered by natives and used as part of the sums paid to the city of Tenochtitlán (Mexico City) by conquered peoples.

Peppers are considered fruit because, like apples and pears, they are seed bearing "packets" of the plant on which they grow. Other such vegetable fruits include tomatoes, eggplants, green beans, cucumbers, and squash. (In some instances, it is the seed, rather than the packet that is eaten, as with peas, lima beans, corn, and other pod and seed vegetables.)

NUTRITION

All peppers are rich in vitamin C and potassium, some are rich in phosphorus, calcium, and niacin. Red and yellow peppers are also a good source of vitamin A. Red hot chiles are highest in vitamins and nutrients. In countries that rely heavily on maize (South America and Africa, for example), peppers help round out the daily diet by supplying valuable nutrients when other fruits are scarce.

Peppers are exceptionally low in calories, averaging about 35 for a large green bell, 50 for a large red bell, 20 for a long green chile (Ancho and Mexi-bell), and 4 for a small chile (jalapeño). They are a good source of fiber and are low in sodium.

THE PEPPER SEASON

Commercially grown peppers are available year-round. The winter supply is grown principally in California, Florida, and Texas with many southern, midwestern, and eastern states growing summer supplies. Most homegrown varieties peak August through October.

The exotic bell peppers — black, orange, yellow — are cultivated primarily in Holland. Grown hydroponically in controlled atmosphere greenhouses, they are prized for their flavor and thick flesh, though they are very perishable. They also cost more than domestic peppers.

PEPPER TIPS

To purchase. Be picky. Look for firm shiny peppers with smooth thick skins. Pale-colored bell peppers are immature and not flavorful. Avoid peppers that are shriveled, wrinkled, blemished, limp, bruised, or soft.

To store. Store fresh peppers in a paper bag or wrap in paper towels and keep refrigerated. Never store peppers in plastic because it retains moisture that causes rot. Green bell peppers will keep up to five days; red bell peppers will keep up to three days. Fresh chiles will keep up to four weeks. Dried peppers will keep indefinitely in a cool dry place.

To freeze. To freeze peppers, blanch for about eight minutes in rapidly boiling water. Do not freeze peppers raw because the bells will lose their crunch and the chiles will loose their bite.

To dry. It's best to dry fresh chiles on a drying rack in the sun. Depending on the size and moisture content, it may take several days to several weeks. Or try stringing chiles together first and hanging outside. Red chiles become a deep burgundy or terra-cotta color and make beautiful gifts strung and dried or attached to wreaths.

When purchasing dried chiles, check them over to be sure they are free of insects. They should have a red glossy color and be free of spots. Remove those that are soft or discolored so they do not infect the others.

Store dried chiles in a cool dry place. Check periodically to remove any that have spoiled. They will keep indefinitely.

PEPPERS BY THE POUND

Weights and measures of individual peppers will vary greatly. The following is an approximate guide:

1 pound bell peppers = 2 – 3 large red, green, yellow, black, or purple bells
1 pound chiles (small) = 6 – 8 jalapeño, serrano, or cherry chiles
1 pound chiles (medium) = 4 – 6 Anaheim, yellow, or Roumanian chiles

1 large bell pepper = 2 cups chopped
              = ½ cup roasted
1 small chile = 2 tablespoons chopped
              = 1 tablespoon roasted
1 medium chile = ⅛ cup chopped
              = 2 tablespoons roasted

SUBSTITUTIONS (in a pinch)

All the recipes in this book call for fresh peppers because the individual flavors and textures of fresh peppers are truly special. However, in a pinch, it's very easy to substitute canned prepared peppers for fresh without greatly altering the results. Just remember that the canned chiles don't pack quite the punch as the fresh.

Here's a quick guide:

- One 3.5-ounce can jalapeño chiles = 2 – 3 fresh jalapeño peppers (the fresh, depending on potency, have more bite). Add more canned jalapeños for a hotter taste.
- One 4-ounce jar pimientos = 1 large roasted bell pepper or ½ cup. Bell peppers (in most recipes) are interchangeable. It is possible to substitute green peppers for any of the bright-colored bells without losing the integrity of the recipe. The taste and, of course, color of the dish will be somewhat different depending on the substitution, but the results should not be disappointing.

PEPPER VARIETIES RANGE in size and flavor and are generally categorized as sweet peppers (mild and crunchy) and chile peppers (wild and spicy). Most green peppers will ripen further if left on the vine, turning red and becoming sweeter. Red peppers are simply green peppers that have been allowed to ripen fully. Many of the green chiles are used fresh, but are dried after they ripen and become red.

Chile peppers are used primarily as a spice adding zip to a variety of dishes from Indian curry to Szechwan pork. The larger, milder varieties may be stuffed, grilled, or sautéed. Unlike bells, chile peppers are generally not eaten out of hand.

Here is a brief guide to the different varieties available in local farmers' markets and supermarkets throughout the country.

SWEET PEPPERS

Aconcagua: This sweet large yellow and red pepper, originally from Argentina, is delicious roasted and peeled.

Anaheim Mild: This is a large long pepper that tastes like a thin-skinned bell and is sold green or red.

Bell: Bell peppers are now available in colors of yellow, deep orange, eggplant purple, and chocolate. All are crunchy with uniquely different flavors.
- Green: snappy and somewhat tart
- Red: sweet
- Yellow: sweeter than red
- Gold: spicy sweet
- Purple: Grassy and turns green when cooked
- Chocolate: somewhat sweet and turns green when cooked

Colorado Mild: This large green or dark red pepper from New Mexico is used roasted and peeled.

Cubanelle: A sweet, medium-size green, red, or yellow pepper, it is used fresh or roasted.

Holland: The light purple and white (yellow) Holland peppers are long, conical, and taste like sweet bell peppers. Though pricy, they add exotic color to a variety of dishes.

Hungarian Red: These have a distinct flavor and are used dried and ground into paprika.

Hungarian Sweet: These long, pointy, yellow wax peppers are sweet and mild and are delicious stuffed.

Italian Frying Peppers: Slender, conical, and thin-walled, these light green or red peppers have a superior taste and are usually sautéed or added to sauces.

Peperoncini: This is a sweet, small pepper, thin-fleshed, green and red and is used mostly for pickling.

Pimientos: These sweet, medium-size peppers are round with a tapered end and generally darker than the red bells. They are often chopped and pickled or used for stuffed green olives. *(Note: The Spanish call any red pepper a pimiento.)*

Roumanian Sweet: Medium-size, thick-fleshed, yellow or red, these are used fresh or canned.

Sweet Cherry: This is a round, medium thin pepper used red and green for pickling.

Ta Tong: A sweet pepper that resembles an elongated bell, it is dark green or red and imported from Japan.

Yellow Petite: This is a sweet, small yellow and red pepper with fine flavor that is used fresh in salads and sauces, or pickled.

Yellow Sweet Wax: This medium thin yellow or red sweet pepper is used fresh or pickled.

CHILE PEPPERS

Anaheim (also known as California green chile, long green chile, New Mexico pepper, California pepper, chile verde, or Rio Grande pepper)**:** This vivid green chile is the mildest of the chile peppers. It is about 7 inches long and 1½ inches wide, with a rounded tip. It is often used in chiles rellenos (stuffed chiles). When grown in California, it tends to be milder than when grown in Mexico.

Bonda Man Jacques: A hot, shriveled, lantern-shaped red pepper from Guadelupe, it is similar to the habanero chiles found in America. The name means Madame Jacque's behind in Creole.

Bird Peppers: These small hot peppers are found in Caribbean pepper sauces and many West Indian dishes. Most often, they are preserved in vinegar or sherry.

Cayenne: This hot, long, thin green and red chile is similar in flavor to jalapeño. It originated in Cayenne

Guiana, South America. In its red ripe state, the dried chile is ground with other chiles to produce cayenne pepper.

College 64L: This mild, medium pepper is used both green and red, fresh, roasted, or dried and powdered.

Fresno: Short and tapered, this chile is very hot and spicy, whether in its green or red ripe state. It is used with care to flavor Mexican and Szechwan sauces and meat. It is grown only in California.

Goldspike: This hot small yellow and red hybrid is thick-fleshed and used in sauces and salads.

Guero: This very hot, yellow chile resembles the size and shape of the jalapeño, about 4 – 5 inches long.

Habanero: A very hot, light green, red, or deep purple chile, it looks like a miniature lantern or small bell pepper. It is used in West African, Latin American, and West Indian cuisine.

Hot Cherry: Larger than the sweet cherry, it's used primarily green and red in pickles.

Jalapeño: Thick-fleshed and cone-shaped with a smooth, deep green skin that can run greenish black. About 2 inches long by 1 inch wide, this is one hot and wild pepper. Jalapeños are probably the most familiar of all chiles because of their use in Mexican and Tex-Mex foods.

Malaguenta: A very hot, bright green and red, 1 inch long chile used in Brazilian cooking. It is available in the United States pickled or preserved in vinegar.

Mexi-bell: A new hybrid of a sweet bell and a spicy chile, the Mexi-bell is milder than the Anaheim and the size of a sweet bell. The "heat" of this chile can be controlled by leaving in or removing the membrane structure along the ribs of the pepper. It is delicious stuffed or added to salads and salsas.

Pequin: A very hot, small, oval, bright red chile about ½ inch long.

Pimiento de Cheiro: A small hot chile used in Brazilian cooking.

Poblano: This is a mild, dark green (almost black) chile with a triangular shape. It is hotter than the Anaheim and a bit bitter. It is delicious stuffed and grilled, served with melted cheese. Ancho is the dried form of Poblano.

Roumanian Hot: This has a medium bell-like shape, and both the red and yellow are used fresh or canned.

Santa Fe Grande: A hot, small yellow-orange or red pepper, it is used fresh or pickled.

Serrano: One hot, hot pepper, the serrano is lighter green in color than the jalapeño, but is sometimes available in red. It is more widely used in Mexico and the southwestern United States than any of the fresh chile peppers, despite the popularity of the jalapeño. It makes "hot" salsa, curry, and meat dishes "hot." Careful as you go.

Tabasco: This very hot, smooth-skinned, light green, and bright red tapered chile averages about 1½ inches long. It is sold bottled whole and fresh. Despite its name, it is not an ingredient in Tabasco sauce which is made of tiny red, green, and yellow peppers that grow *only* in the salty soil of Avery Island, New Iberia, Louisiana.

Takanostume: This hot, thin, tiny pepper from Japan is used red and green in fresh sauces.

Tuscan: Small, light green, and hot, this pepper is pickled in brine for use in Italian salads and antipasto dishes.

Wiri-wiri: This hot, small, cherry-like, red skinned chile is native to Guiana, where home cooks grow them in pots on windowsills.

Yellow Chile (varieties include yellow wax, Hungarian or Armenian wax, floral gem, banana pepper, or caribe)**:** Favored by Cajun cooks, tapering pale and somewhat plump, these yellow peppers are native to Louisiana and have a mild but spicy bite. These are often pickled. It's nearly impossible to know their degree of hotness without tasting first.

Yung Ko: A hot, long, slender, curved pepper used fresh in its dark green or red ripe state.

DRIED CHILE PEPPERS

Ancho Chile: The most commonly used dried pepper in Mexico, the Ancho is known as the Poblano in its fresh state. It measures about 5 inches long and 3 inches wide, has a wrinkled appearance, and a deep mahogany color. It's most commonly used in adobo (a marinade for chicken), in a chile-flavored dough for quesadillas, and in a red chile sauce.

Cascabel: A mild, hot, small pepper of reddish brown, its name means "little bell."

Chile de Árbol: A cayenne-type pepper, this vibrant orange, red dried chile measures 3 inches long and tapers to a sharp point. It is very hot with a vicious bite.

Mulato: A mild, hot medium-size pepper with reddish black skin.

New Mexico Chile: This is a dried Anaheim, both mild and hot. It's a large, long tapering chile with smooth skin of red brick to oxblood. Most often it's first soaked, then used in Mexican and Indian recipes.

Pasilla: This long, hot, slender pepper is dark red and chocolate brown. It gives sauces a rich distinctive flavor.

COOKING WITH PEPPERS

A special note about chiles — Cooks, be careful!

Chiles contain volatile oils that can irritate and burn skin and eyes. Wear rubber gloves when working with chiles and be sure not to touch your face or eyes. Wash your hands thoroughly with warm, soapy water when finished. If you can't work in rubber gloves, rub your hands with cooking oil before handling, to help protect your skin.

Should you suffer from chile burn (that begins with a tingling irritation), soak the affected area in milk. Sugar will also help neutralize burns. If your eyes or nose are burned by chiles, flush immediately with cold water.

When working with dried chiles, use only cold water. Hot water poured on dried chiles may produce fumes that can irritate nose and eyes.

LOWERING THE HEAT

The chile's heat is contained in its veins, not as once believed, in the seeds. Devein and seed chiles before using.

Here are some tips for lowering a hot pepper's thermostat:

- Soak fresh chiles in cold water, or in a 5 to 1 water to vinegar mixture for 45 minutes.
- Place chiles in a pot of cold water, bring to a boil, then let stand for 2 – 3 minutes before draining.
- To temper dried chile sauces, add paprika and increase the use of tomato sauce.
- Add red or green bell pepper puree to chile sauces that may be too hot.
- Use hot peppers wisely and according to taste.

PEPPER PRODUCTS

Look for these peppery condiments in gourmet and specialty stores (recipes for making your own are noted).

Cayenne: This hot powder is made from various dried chiles (mostly cayenne chiles). It ranges in color from terra-cotta to deep maroon depending on the blend of chiles. The flavor may range from pungent to smoky.

Chile Powder: Chile powders vary from mildly hot to very hot depending on the brand. Most commercial brands are mild and contain a mixture of dried chile powder, garlic, cumin, oregano, and salt. Specialty brands usually have stronger flavors and bolder characters.

Chile Sauce: Most commercial sauces contain a small amount of chile powder and lots of tomato sauce and horseradish with a bit of garlic. Homemade or specialty chile sauce is likely to be fresh tasting and piquant.

Curry Powder: Does not exist in India. Cooks combine their own blend of freshly roasted and ground peppercorns, dried chiles, turmeric, cardamom, coriander, mustard, and cumin. The commercial curry powders contain a variety of these spices and should be used according to taste.

Harissa: A very hot paste used to flavor Tunisian couscous, it is made of pulverized dried chile peppers, cumin, and salt.

Hot Pepper Oil: A mixture of hot chile peppers and oil is very hot and adds kick to a variety of Szechwan and Hunan dishes. (See recipe on page 134.)

Louisiana Red and Green Sauces: Sold in long narrow bottles, these hot, hot sauces are made from a variety of hot chiles, vinegar, sugar, and miscellaneous spices.

Paprika: Paprika peppers are dried and ground into powder, adding unique flavor and color to a variety of dishes. Hungarian paprika is considered the most flavorful and vivid paprika.

Peperoncini: Pickled, hot Tuscan peppers packaged in brine, peperoncini is used in Italian antipasto dishes.

Pickapeppa Sauce: A Jamaican condiment similar to Worcestershire sauce, pickapeppa sauce is made of hot peppers, sugar, salt, and spices and is very hot.

Pickled Peppers: Small red and green chiles, cured in vinegar, pickled peppers are a common condiment of Cajun, Creole, and soul food tables, adding bite to any dish. The flavorful liquid is used to add zest to soups and stews and can be replenished by adding cider vinegar to the jar. (See recipe on page 137)

Pimiento: Skinned, roasted red bell peppers, pimientos are used as garnishes and in a variety of Spanish and Portuguese dishes. Pimientos may be substituted for roasted red peppers in most recipes.

Pizza Peppers: A mixture of dried chiles, pizza peppers are named for the pie to which they add spice.

Recaito: This mild condiment is made of coriander, onion, garlic, and red bell pepper and used in Puerto Rican cooking.

Ristras (Chile Wreath): The Ristra is a traditional symbol of hope and plenty in Mexico and the American Southwest. There, dried chiles were added to staple foods (corn, polenta, beans) for storage during the winter. It acted as a preservative and added flavor and taste. The chile pods were strung to hasten drying in the autumn sun, and to keep them above the reach of scavengers. Keep in a cool dry area away from excessive heat or moisture. Do not refrigerate.

Tabasco Sauce: This patented and aged blend of vinegar, spices, and tiny red, green, and yellow hot peppers which grow in the salty soil of Avery Island in New Iberia, Louisiana, is a prerequisite for the perfect Bloody Mary.

Schichimitogarashi: This is a common Japanese condiment of ground red hot peppers, sesame, mustard, and poppy seeds, dried tangerine peel, rape seed, and Japanese pepper leaf. It is present on most Japanese tables.

Sofrito: Bell peppers, onions, tomatoes, pork, and a variety of spices are combined in this condiment that figures in much Hispanic cooking: fricasses, stews, asapao, etc.

HERE IS A SELECTION of quick and easy basic pepper preparation suggestions and serving ideas.

ROASTED PEPPERS

Roasted bell peppers have a unique sweet and smoky flavor. They are delicious by themselves or marinated in olive oil and a little vinegar. Covered and refrigerated, they will store approximately five days.

Roasting chile peppers tempers their heat and gives a special dimension to dishes calling for chiles. The technique for roasting bells and chiles is the same.

Place whole pepper under a broiler, on an open grill, or hold over a gas flame with tongs. Turn frequently until the skin is charred and blistered (about 20 – 30 minutes). Place peppers in a paper bag or wrap in paper towels for about 15 – 30 minutes. This will steam them and help loosen the skins. Using a sharp knife, pull back the skin, (some of it may simply rub off with a paper towel). Cut peppers and discard veins and seeds.

SAUTÉED PEPPERS

For each pound of sweet peppers (deveined, seeded, and sliced), melt 2 tablespoons of butter, margarine, or olive oil (alone or in combination) over medium heat. Add peppers and cook, stirring frequently about 10 – 15 minutes or until tender.

STIR-FRIED

For each pound of sweet peppers (deveined, seeded, and sliced), melt 2 tablespoons peanut or vegetable oil (alone or in combination) in a wok or a large skillet set over high heat. Stir-fry 1 minute, add 2 tablespoons stock or water, cover, and cook 3 minutes, or until peppers are just tender.

MY SISTER AND I share a passion for the piquant,
a taste my husband approaches with caution. When Suzie
and I get together, we explore the hot and wild flavors in Thai,
Vietnamese, Indian, Szechwan, Spanish, and Latin American
eateries, often making an entire meal of the "small plates" and
appetizers. Whether we meet in San Francisco, Suzie's
New York, or my Minneapolis, the fun is in tasting
new flavors and textures while sharing the "hot stuff"
of gossip and men, memories, and dreams.

The appetizers offered here will perk up the palate
with color, texture, and interesting flavors. Zesty *Hungarian
Hot Pepper Cheese* on crisp crackers, *Jazzed Baked Oysters*,
and *Peppery Nuts* are nibbles of Mexican, Latin American,
Creole, and African flavors.

Many of these may be offered as selections
with cocktails or in several small courses to make a
full meal. Today's tastes run toward smaller portions
of different foods offering tempting variety with tapas and
finger-size fare. Be generous with fresh vegetables, herbs,
and interesting garnishes. Mix and match selections for light,
festive entertaining and elegant everyday style.

ROASTED HERBED PEPPERS

PREPARATION TIME: 15 MINUTES
MAKES: 2 CUPS

4 medium red, yellow, or orange bell
   peppers, roasted and peeled (see
   page 10)
1 clove garlic, minced
1 tablespoon olive oil
1 tablespoon balsamic vinegar
   or red wine vinegar
2 tablespoons freshly chopped mint, or
   other fresh herb like basil, tarragon,
   oregano, cilantro, alone or in
   combination

This is a very versatile dish.

Devein and seed the peppers, slice into strips. In a small bowl, combine the peppers with the remaining ingredients.

SERVE:
• with cream cheese and crisp crackers.
• on top of Focaccia and goat cheese.
• as a side to grilled chicken or to top hamburgers.
• spread on a sandwich of spicy ham and mild cheddar.
• spread over crusty French bread, topped with mozzarella cheese and broiled.

PROVENÇALE PEPPERS

PREPARATION TIME: 1 HOUR
MAKES: 2 CUPS

¼ cup olive oil
2 tablespoons butter
2 cups chopped onions
1 *each* medium red and yellow bell
   pepper, deveined and seeded,
   thinly sliced
2 cloves garlic, minced
½ cup freshly shredded basil leaves
   or parsley
Salt and freshly ground black pepper
   to taste

In a large saucepan, heat the oil and butter. Add the onions and peppers and simmer about 45 minutes over low heat, or until the vegetables are limp and tender. (This should have a marmalade-like appearance.)

Add the garlic and basil and cook 5 minutes. Remove from the heat and allow to cool to room temperature. Drain excess oil.

These sweet and tangy peppers, inspired by the pungent herbs and mellow olive oils from Provence, France, make quick and versatile appetizers. Try these for starters.

- Serve with crisp crackers, bagel or pita chips.
- Use as a filling for little quiche crusts or mini-puff pastry shells.
- Serve with a crock of *Hungarian Hot Pepper Cheese.*
(See page 31.)
- Broil mozzarella and Parmesan cheese on small slices of French bread and top with *Provençale Peppers.*

PEPPER TORTILLAS

PREPARATION TIME: 10 MINUTES
SERVES: 14

½ cup olive oil
1 large red bell pepper, deveined and
   seeded, thinly sliced
1 Italian frying pepper, deveined and
   seeded, thinly sliced
1 Holland or cubanelle pepper,
   deveined and seeded, thinly sliced
3 cloves garlic, minced
3 jalapeño peppers, deveined and
   seeded
14 small 6-inch tortillas
Guacamole (see page 26)
Sour cream

These fiery sautéed peppers are also terrific on tacos, tortillas, and nachos.

In a large skillet or wok, heat the oil and sauté the peppers and garlic for 3 minutes. Add the whole jalapeños and cook another 3 minutes. Spoon the mixture into warmed tortillas and top with the guacamole and sour cream.

PEPPER BACLAZANA

PREPARATION TIME: 30 MINUTES
STANDING TIME: 2 HOURS
SERVES: 8

½ cup olive oil
3 *each* medium red and green bell
    peppers, deveined and seeded,
    coarsely chopped
1 cup chopped onions
1 large eggplant, peeled and cut into
    ¼-inch cubes
½ cup chopped celery
½ cup dry white wine
1 teaspoon sugar
¼ teaspoon chile powder
Salt and freshly ground black
    pepper to taste
3 tablespoons capers

The marvelous flavors of peppers and spices need time to marry. This spread tastes best the day after it's made. Serve with a light, dry white wine and a mild goat cheese.

In a large skillet or wok, heat the oil and add the vegetables. Cook over low heat, stirring frequently, 30 minutes. Add the wine, sugar, chile powder, salt, and pepper. Cook 15 minutes. Add the capers and check the seasonings.

Turn into a bowl, cover, and refrigerate at least 2 hours or overnight. Serve with small slices of rye, pumpernickel, or country French bread.

PREPARATION TIME: 20 MINUTES
SERVES: 10

1-2 jalapeño peppers, deveined and
    seeded, chopped
1 medium red bell pepper, deveined
    and seeded, chopped
1 tablespoon vegetable oil
¼ pound butter, softened
1 cup mayonnaise
½ pound Monterey Jack cheese,
    grated
2 small loaves French bread, sliced
    into ¼-inch slices
Fresh cilantro or parsley for garnish

No one knows who Josephina was, but this recipe is memorable. Serve as is for a hearty appetizer or as a companion to homemade soups and stews.

Preheat the broiler. In a small saucepan, sauté the peppers in the oil over medium-high heat until soft. Drain excess oil. In a medium-size bowl, combine the butter, mayonnaise, and cheese. Stir in the peppers. Spread the bread slices with the cheese mixture, completely covering the bread. Place on an ungreased baking sheet and broil 7–10 minutes or until bubbly. Garnish with the cilantro or parsley.

PEPPERS STUFFED WITH TOMATOES AND HERBED CHEESE

PREPARATION TIME: 15 MINUTES
BAKING TIME: 40 MINUTES
SERVES: 8 TO 16

4 large red or green bell peppers, tops
    removed and reserved, cored and
    seeded, but left whole
One 8-ounce package cream cheese,
    cut into 4 pieces
¼ cup freshly chopped parsley
¼ cup freshly chopped basil
2 medium tomatoes, coarsely chopped
2 tablespoons olive oil, divided
Salt and freshly ground black pepper
    to taste
½ cup white wine

This lovely, easy first course also makes an impressive side dish.

Preheat over to 350°F. Cut a thin slice from the bottom of each pepper so it will stand upright. Press a piece of cream cheese into the bottom of each pepper, sprinkle with the parsley and basil, then the tomatoes. Sprinkle with the oil, salt, and pepper. Replace the tops on the peppers.

Rub the outside of the peppers with the oil and place in a shallow baking dish. Pour the wine into the bottom of the dish. Bake about 40 minutes or until tender. To serve, slice each pepper in half or quarters. Be careful that the stuffing is divided equally.

PEPPER BOATS ITALIANO

PREPARATION TIME: 40 MINUTES
BAKING TIME: 25-30 MINUTES
SERVES: 6 TO 8

4 medium red bell peppers, roasted
   and peeled (see page 10)
½ cup fresh bread crumbs
1 cup freshly shredded mozzarella
   cheese
½ cup freshly shredded provolone
   cheese
¼ cup capers
¼ cup chopped walnuts
¼ cup chopped black olives
¼ cup freshly chopped Italian or
   flat parsley
1 clove garlic, minced
Salt and freshly ground black pepper
   to taste
1 tablespoon olive oil

These are hearty appetizers, best offered prior to a light meal.

Preheat oven to 350°F. Devein and seed the peppers. Slice lengthwise in half and place close together in a well-greased baking dish.

In a small bowl, combine the remaining ingredients and distribute evenly into the pepper halves. Bake 25 – 30 minutes or until bubbly. Serve hot or at room temperature.

PEPPERY MINI-PIZZAS

PREPARATION TIME: 15 MINUTES
BAKING TIME: 10 MINUTES
SERVES: 8

4 tablespoons olive oil
½ cup minced onions
1 cup tomato sauce
2 cloves garlic, minced
½ teaspoon pizza pepper spice
2 tablespoons freshly chopped
  oregano, or 1 teaspoon dried
¼ cup freshly chopped basil,
  or 3 teaspoons dried
1 cup sliced mushrooms
1 *each* medium red and green
  bell pepper, diced
8 mini-pita bread pockets, divided
  in half
¾ cup freshly grated mozzarella
  cheese
¼ cup freshly grated Romano cheese

Peppers are the new trend in jewelry, art, clothes, and even ice cream. Sebastain Joe's Ice Cream Parlor, Franklin Avenue, Minneapolis, sometimes features Mexican Chocolate Cha Cha ice cream. This blend of rich imported chocolate and smooth midwest cream is made spicy with freshly ground cinnamon and dried chiles. It tastes like a chocolate-covered "Red Hot" candy.

Preheat oven to 350°F. In a heavy, medium-size saucepan, heat *2 tablespoons oil* and sauté the onions over medium heat until transparent, about 5 minutes. Add the tomato sauce, garlic, pizza pepper, oregano, and basil and stir to combine. Simmer about 5 minutes to thicken.

In a medium-size skillet, heat the remaining oil and sauté the mushrooms and peppers until tender, about 5 minutes. Set aside.

Place the pitas on a baking sheet and bake about 4 minutes or until crisp. Spread the sauce equally over each pita, distributing it evenly. Sprinkle each pita with equal amounts of both cheeses. Top with the reserved peppers and mushrooms. Return to the oven and bake about 5 minutes, or until the cheese is melted and bubbly.

GRILLED SHRIMP WITH PEPPERS AND PROSCIUTTO

PREPARATION TIME: 20 MINUTES
SERVES: 6 TO 8

½ cup white wine
½ cup olive oil
3 tablespoons fresh lemon juice
1 tablespoon Dijon mustard
3 tablespoons freshly chopped basil
12 raw jumbo shrimp, peeled and
    deveined
2 large red or yellow bell peppers,
    deveined and seeded, cut into 8
    strips (about the size of the shrimp)
12 thin slices prosciutto, fat trimmed

These tasty shrimp also make a lovely light supper served on a bed of herbed rice. This will serve four for supper.

In a medium-size glass bowl, combine the wine, oil, lemon juice, mustard, and basil and pour over the shrimp. Marinate at least 3 hours or overnight.

Prepare the grill for hot coals. Remove the shrimp and reserve the marinade. Place a shrimp and slice of pepper together and wrap with a piece of prosciutto. Thread on metal skewers, placing additional slices of pepper at the top and bottom of skewer.

Grill the shrimp, basting frequently with the marinade for 2 minutes per side or until pink. Serve immediately.

JAZZED BAKED OYSTERS

PREPARATION TIME: 20 MINUTES
SERVES: 4

24 large oysters, shucked (retain
    liquor and reserve half shell)
¾ cup Pernod
2 cups white wine
1 tablespoon *Hot Pepper Oil* (see
    page 134)
2 tablespoons minced chives
¼ cup *each* minced red and green
    bell pepper
3 tablespoons drained and minced
    green peppercorns
½ teaspoon crushed dried chile

New Orleans is the home of jazz and all manner of baked oysters: Oysters Rockefeller, Oysters Sardou, and Oysters Roffignac.

Preheat oven to 350°F. Place the oysters on their half shells in a shallow roasting pan and pour *2 teaspoons Pernod* and *1 tablespoon wine* onto each. Cover tightly with aluminum foil and bake 10 minutes. In a small saucepan, combine all the remaining ingredients and heat through, stirring constantly. Place the oysters on a serving dish and pour the sauce over all. Serve immediately.

CHILE PEPPER EMPANADITAS

PREPARATION TIME: 1 HOUR
BAKING TIME: 25 MINUTES
SERVES: 10 TO 15

These pretty pastry packets make impressive appetizers.

Filling

½ pound skinless, boneless chicken
   or turkey breast meat
2 tablespoons olive oil
10 green pitted olives
3 green Italian frying peppers,
   deveined and seeded, chopped
¼ cup dry white wine
1 clove garlic, minced
1 teaspoon ground cumin
Salt and freshly ground black pepper
   to taste
½ cup freshly chopped cilantro or
   parsley
2 tablespoons butter
1 jalapeño pepper, deveined and
   seeded, thinly sliced
Fresh cilantro for garnish

FILLING

   Slice the chicken or turkey into thin strips. In a medium-size skillet, sauté the meat in the oil over medium heat about 4 minutes or until no longer pink. Set aside.

   In a blender or food processor fitted with the steel blade, puree the olives and Italian peppers until smooth. Add the puree to the sautéed chicken, then add the wine, garlic, cumin, salt, and pepper. Return this chicken mixture to the skillet and cook over medium heat, about 30 minutes. Add the cilantro, butter, and jalapeño and continue cooking another 5 minutes. Set aside.

DOUGH

   Preheat oven to 375°F. Combine the flour with the sugar and salt. Cut in the butter with a pastry cutter or fingers until the mixture resembles small peas. (This may also be done with a food processor fitted with the steel blade, processing mixture quickly with on-off switch.) Combine the egg and ice water and gradually add to the flour and butter mixture, stirring with a fork until the ingredients are combined. Turn onto a lightly floured

(continued)

(continued)

Dough
2½ cups all-purpose flour
1 teaspoon sugar
1 teaspoon salt
¼ pound butter
1 egg
½ cup ice water

surface and gently knead until the mixture holds together. Wrap in plastic and place in the refrigerator about 10 minutes.

On a lightly floured surface, roll out the dough to ⅛ inch thick. Cut into 2 ½-inch rounds using a biscuit cutter or glass. Put 2 teaspoons of the filling in each round. Wet the edges with water and fold the pastry in half. Press the edges firmly all around with the tongs of a fork. Place on a greased baking sheet and refrigerate until ready to bake. Brush with a glaze of 1 egg mixed with 1 tablespoon water. Bake 25 minutes or until golden brown. Garnish with the cilantro.

Empanaditas may be made in advance and frozen (unbaked), then baked in a 375°F. oven 35–40 minutes. Do not thaw before baking.

PEPPER PHYLLO PACKETS

PREPARATION TIME: 30 MINUTES
CHILLING TIME: 1 HOUR
BAKING TIME: 20 MINUTES
SERVES: 8 TO 10

Filling
¼ cup olive oil
2 pounds red and green bell peppers, deveined and seeded, coarsely chopped
1 small onion, chopped
1 clove garlic, minced
¼ cup freshly chopped basil, or 1 tablespoon dried
2 tablespoons freshly chopped oregano, or 2 teaspoons dried
¼ cup freshly grated Parmesan cheese
¼ cup freshly grated mozzarella cheese

Phyllo
½ pound phyllo dough
1 cup melted butter

FILLING
In a medium-size skillet, heat the oil over medium heat and sauté the peppers, onion, and garlic until just soft. Stir in the herbs and cook about 10–15 minutes, or until the liquid evaporates. Add the cheeses and gently toss to combine.

PHYLLO
To prepare the phyllo, lay it flat and cut lengthwise into 5-inch strips. Stack the strips and cover with a damp towel. Remove a layer of dough and replace the towel on the stack so that the dough will stay moist and fresh. Brush the layer with melted butter (use pastry brush or small, soft new paint brush). Place the second layer on top of the first and brush with the butter, remembering to recover the phyllo stack with the towel.

Spoon 2 tablespoons of filling about two inches from one end of the buttered strips of phyllo. Fold in the side edges about ½ inch until just barely covering the filling. Then fold the tail of the phyllo over the filling just to cover, and butter. Now that the filling is covered by one fold, fold up again and butter. Continue folding the phyllo around the filling, buttering after each fold. Continue this process until the filling is used up.

Preheat oven to 375°F. Place folded packets in a single layer in a shallow baking pan or on a baking sheet lined with

(continued)

PEPPER PHYLLO PACKETS (continued)

aluminum foil and greased. Chill at least 1 hour or overnight. Bake the packets about 20 minutes or until golden brown. These impressive appetizers may be made ahead and frozen instead of chilled. Do not thaw before baking. Simply place on a greased baking sheet while still frozen and bake in a preheated 375°F. oven 40 minutes or until brown.

CAL-MEX QUESADILLAS

PREPARATION TIME: 15 MINUTES
SERVES: 8

¼ pound butter, softened
Salt and freshly ground black pepper
   to taste
12 flour tortillas
1 cup freshly grated Monterey Jack
   cheese
1 cup freshly grated mozzarella cheese
2 Anaheim chiles, deveined and
   seeded, chopped

These spicy, cheesy appetizers combine California peppers with a popular Mexican appetizer.

Preheat the broiler. Lightly butter and salt and pepper both sides of the tortillas. Place the tortillas on an ungreased baking sheet. Cover the tortillas equally first with the cheeses, then the Anaheim chiles. Broil 5-8 minutes, or until the cheese is bubbly and golden brown. Remove from the oven and cut into wedges.

GUACAMOLE
(Hot Mexican or Cool Californian)

PREPARATION TIME: 20 MINUTES
MAKES: 2 CUPS

1 small onion, finely chopped, divided
1 or 2 serrano chiles, deveined and
   seeded, chopped
4 tablespoons freshly chopped cilantro
2 large very ripe avocados, peeled
   and pitted
1 large tomato, peeled, seeded, and
   chopped
Salt and freshly ground black pepper
   to taste
Fresh cilantro for garnish

The word guacamole comes from the Mexican words for avocado and mixture. In Mexico, guacamole is eaten at the beginning of the meal with warm tortillas. It is also served with rice or tacos as a side dish.

HOT MEXICAN GUACAMOLE

In a blender or food processor fitted with the steel blade, process one-half of the onion with the chiles and cilantro into a smooth paste. (Traditionally this is done with a molcajete, or mortar and pestle.)

In a separate bowl, mash the avocados with the back of a fork or molcajete and add the chile paste. Stir in the tomato and remaining onion, salt, and pepper. Garnish with the cilantro and serve immediately.

Note: This is a very delicate guacamole, best eaten right after it's made. The delicate green of the avocado turns dark in no time.

COOL CALIFORNIAN GUACAMOLE

Substitute 1 Anaheim chile (deveined and seeded) chopped, for the serrano chile. Add 1 additional large tomato, 1 teaspoon cumin, and ½ cup sour cream to the recipe. Garnish with chopped tomatoes and chopped cilantro.

INDIAN PEPPER AND MINT DIP

PREPARATION TIME: 15 MINUTES
MAKES: 2 CUPS

1 cup plain low-fat yogurt
1 jalapeño pepper, deveined and
   seeded
4 scallions, chopped (including green
   tops)
1 tablespoon chopped fresh ginger
¼ cup freshly chopped mint
½ cup freshly chopped cilantro

This dip is traditionally served with poppadoms, flat crisp wafers made from chick-pea flour. A staple of the Indian table, poppadoms are plain or spiced with black pepper or chile powder. They are eaten as an appetizer or an accompaniment to curry dishes. Poppadoms are complicated to make at home, but they are available from specialty food stores.

Process all the ingredients in a blender or food processor fitted with the steel blade until the mixture is creamy. Pour into a small bowl and refrigerate at least 1 hour. Serve with Indian poppadoms and slices of fresh bell pepper.

PREPARATION TIME: 10 MINUTES
MAKES: 1 CUP

½ cup peanut butter
2 tablespoons water
4 tablespoons soy sauce
¼ cup dark sesame oil
2 tablespoons sherry
4 teaspoons rice wine vinegar
¼ cup honey
4 cloves garlic, minced
3 teaspoons minced fresh ginger
2 tablespoons *Hot Pepper Oil* (see
    page 134)
Chopped peanuts for garnish

Serve vegetable dips in hollowed out peppers for a startling presentation. Use red, purple, and yellow peppers in the center of a large plate and surround with strips of fresh bell peppers and lots of colorful vegetables.

In a blender or food processor fitted with the steel blade, combine all the ingredients, except the peanuts, and process until smooth. Thin with hot water, one tablespoon at a time if necessary. Garnish with the peanuts.

FIERY CRAB DIP

PREPARATION TIME: 15 MINUTES
SERVES: 12

½ medium onion, finely chopped
¼ cup peanut oil
2 stalks celery, finely chopped
5 serrano or jalapeño chiles, deveined
   and seeded, chopped
1 cup cooked, shredded crab meat
4 tablespoons freshly chopped cilantro
Salt and freshly ground black pepper
   to taste

Try the new frozen surimi (natural imitation crab meat made with white fish) instead of crab.

In a medium-size skillet, sauté the onion in the oil until soft. Add the celery, chiles, and crab meat and cook until celery is tender crisp. Add the cilantro and cook 1 minute more. Salt and pepper to taste. Serve with tortillas or as a dip for chips.

CHILE CON QUESO

PREPARATION TIME: 15 MINUTES
SERVES: 8

1 pound Monterey Jack cheese, shredded
2 tablespoons cornstarch
1 clove garlic, crushed
6 slices bacon
½ cup chopped onions
2 medium tomatoes, chopped
1 small jalapeño pepper, deveined and seeded, diced
½ cup dry white wine

This rich and spicy Mexican fondue makes for a warming start to a winter party.

In a small bowl, combine the cheese with the cornstarch and garlic. In a large skillet, cook the bacon and drain on paper towels. Add the onions to the skillet and lightly sauté. Add the tomatoes and jalapeño and gently stir together the ingredients. Add the wine to the skillet and heat until the mixture comes to a boil. Lower the heat and gradually add the cheese mixture, blending carefully. Do not allow the mixture to boil. Turn the ingredients into a chafing dish or fondue pot set over low heat. Chop the bacon and sprinkle over the cheese. Serve with tortilla chips and slices of colorful bell peppers.

HUNGARIAN HOT PEPPER CHEESE

PREPARATION TIME: 10 MINUTES
SERVES: 8

1 jalapeño pepper, deveined and
  seeded
1 clove garlic
One 8-ounce package cream cheese
2 tablespoons Hungarian paprika
Freshly ground black pepper to taste

This is delicious served with bread sticks, on top of baked potatoes instead of sour cream or butter, or in a sandwich with boiled ham.

In a blender or food processor fitted with the steel blade, process the pepper and garlic until minced. Add the remaining ingredients and process until thoroughly combined. Turn into a decorative crock and serve with slices of fresh bell peppers and crisp crackers.

AFRICAN EGGS DIABLO

PREPARATION TIME: 15 MINUTES
SERVES: 6

6 hard-cooked eggs
¼ cup mayonnaise
1 hot chile pepper (jalapeño or
  habanero), deveined and seeded
1 teaspoon prepared mustard
1 tablespoon ketchup
Paprika for garnish

Hot and spicy peppers play a large role in African cooking. In Ghana, a "good" pepper makes the eater break out in a sweat.

Peel the eggs and cut in half lengthwise. Remove the yolks and reserve the whites. In a small bowl, mix the remaining ingredients until smooth. Distribute the mixture evenly into the egg white shells. Garnish with the paprika.

CARIBBEAN COCONUT (SOUSKAI)

PREPARATION TIME: 10 MINUTES
SERVES: 8

1 ripe coconut, shelled and peeled
2 teaspoons salt
2 cloves garlic, minced
1 Fresno chile, deveined and seeded,
   minced
Juice of 4 limes

In Martinique, this tart and tangy Coconut Souskai makes a delightful complement to the sweet punches and cocktail combinations traditionally served at the end of the day.

Using a potato peeler, sharp knife, or the slicing blade of a food processor, slice the coconut meat into thin strips. Combine the salt, garlic, chile, and lime juice. Marinate the coconut in this mixture for at least 1 hour. Serve with plenty of napkins and optional toothpicks.

PEPPERY NUTS

PREPARATION TIME: 10 MINUTES
MAKES: 2 CUPS

1 cup *each* unsalted cashews and
   unsalted peanuts
1 tablespoon butter
1 teaspoon powdered red chiles or
   cayenne powder
½ teaspoon ground cumin
1¼ teaspoons salt

These make a terrific and easy holiday or hostess gift presented in a pretty jar.

In a medium-size skillet, sauté the nuts in the butter about 10 minutes, stirring frequently to prevent burning. Remove the nuts from the pan and drain on paper towels. Blend the spices and salt and put in a paper bag with the nuts. Shake to coat. Serve warm.

AS A PENNILESS GRADUATE student at the University of New Hampshire, I shared a house with four adventuresome cooks. Given our skinny budget and eclectic tastes, we learned to make much ado of very little.

Shelia, a 6-foot tall, lusty brunette who wore high-heeled boots and long black capes, created hearty batches of soups as dramatic as she. Sheila did not tolerate mild flavors or weak prose. Her bold concoctions were chocked with country vegetables, lots of garlic, and heated with a fiery chile or two.

In the fall, *Shelia's Pumpkin and Roasted Pepper Soup* drew neighbors, professors, and classmates to casual suppers that lasted long into those cool October nights.

RED GAZPACHO

PREPARATION TIME: 10 MINUTES
CHILLING TIME: 4 HOURS
SERVES: 8 TO 10

½ cup red wine vinegar
½ cup olive oil
1 cup V-8 juice
5 large tomatoes, cored and
    chopped; juice reserved
4 medium red bell peppers (or mixture
    of red and orange), deveined and
    seeded, chopped
1 large red Bermuda onion, chopped
2 medium cucumbers, peeled,
    seeded, and chopped
Dash of cayenne powder to taste
Salt and freshly ground black pepper
    to taste
¼ cup freshly chopped basil
Seasoned croutons for garnish

Gazpacho is a native of southern Spain where every cook has a different version depending on family traditions and local produce. Try your own variations on this "vegetable soup-salad." It makes for a cool supper on a hot summer night, served with a basket of dark country bread or corn muffins and a plate of fruit and cheese.

In a small bowl, whisk together the vinegar, olive oil, and V-8 juice. In a blender or food processor fitted with the steel blade, puree the vegetables in batches, adding the V-8 juice mixture as needed. (Do not overprocess, soup should be crunchy.) Turn the pureed batches into a medium-size bowl. Add the cayenne powder, salt, and pepper, and stir in the basil. Cover the bowl and refrigerate 4 hours. Serve in chilled mugs garnished with the croutons.

GREEN GAZPACHO

PREPARATION TIME: 15 MINUTES
CHILLING TIME: 4 HOURS
SERVES: 8

2 cups plain low-fat yogurt
1 cup olive oil
½ cup white wine vinegar
1 bunch scallions, rinsed and coarsely
    chopped
2 stalks celery, coarsely chopped
6 medium green bell peppers,
    deveined and seeded, coarsely
    chopped
2 medium cucumbers, peeled, seeded,
    and coarsely chopped
6 cups rinsed and coarsely chopped
    romaine lettuce leaves
1 clove garlic, minced
Salt and freshly ground black pepper
    to taste
Dash of Tabasco sauce
½ cup freshly chopped dill

In a small bowl, whisk together the yogurt, olive oil, and vinegar. In a blender or food processor fitted with the steel blade, process the vegetables in batches, adding the yogurt mixture. Be careful not to overprocess. Soup should be crunchy. Turn into a medium-size bowl and season with the salt, pepper, and Tabasco. Stir in the dill. Cover and chill 4 hours. Serve in chilled mugs.

FIRE AND ICE GAZPACHO

PREPARATION TIME: 20 MINUTES
CHILLING TIME: 4 HOURS
SERVES: 10

2 cups fresh bread crumbs
3 cloves garlic, minced
1 medium cucumber, peeled, seeded, and diced
3 medium red bell peppers, deveined and seeded, diced
3 jalapeño peppers, deveined and seeded, diced
1 medium onion, chopped
5 medium tomatoes, seeded and diced
5 cups V-8 juice
½ cup fresh lime juice
½ cup olive oil
1 tablespoon ground cumin
1 tablespoon Hungarian paprika
Salt and freshly ground black pepper to taste
2 very ripe avocados, pitted, peeled, and diced
Fresh cilantro for garnish

Besides the fiery bite, chiles are a potent source of vitamins A and C. One two-ounce chile has more than twice the daily requirement of vitamin A established by the federal government.

In a small bowl, combine the bread crumbs and garlic. In a large bowl, combine the cucumber, peppers, onion, tomatoes, V-8 juice, and lime juice. Add the bread crumb mixture and stir in the oil, cumin, and paprika. In a blender or food processor fitted with the steel blade, puree half of the soup. Then, pour the pureed soup back into the bowl with the soup mixture and combine. Salt and pepper to taste. Chill the soup and stir in the avocado just before serving. Garnish with the cilantro.

RED PEPPER SOUP WITH YELLOW PEPPER PUREE

PREPARATION TIME: 45 MINUTES
SERVES: 4 TO 6

Red Pepper Soup
2 tablespoons butter
1 medium onion, chopped
2 cloves garlic, minced
4 medium red bell peppers, roasted
   and peeled (see page 10),
   deveined and seeded, chopped
2 tablespoons all-purpose flour
2 cups chicken stock
¾ cup heavy cream
Salt and freshly ground black pepper
   to taste
Fresh basil for garnish

Yellow Pepper Puree
2 medium yellow bell peppers, roasted
   and peeled (see page 10), deveined
   and seeded, chopped
1 clove garlic, minced
Dash of Tabasco sauce
Salt and freshly ground black pepper to
   taste

The pale colors in this mellow soup make it a favorite of restaurant chefs. When in a hurry, omit the Yellow Pepper Puree.

In a medium-size saucepan set over low-medium heat, melt the butter and sauté the onion and garlic until transparent. Add the peppers and cook 5 minutes. Stir in the flour and cook approximately 2 minutes (do not brown).

Slowly whisk in the chicken stock and bring the mixture to a boil. Reduce the heat and simmer gently 20 minutes. In a blender or food processor fitted with the steel blade, puree the pepper mixture until smooth. Return the mixture to the saucepan. Whisk in the cream and cook until heated through (do not boil). Salt and pepper to taste.

PUREE
In a blender or food processor fitted with the steel blade, puree all the ingredients and season to taste.

To serve
Ladle the soup into individual serving bowls. Add 2 tablespoons *Yellow Pepper Puree* into each and cut through with a knife to create swirls. Garnish with the basil. Soup may be served hot or cold.

VICHYSSOISE
WITH RED AND YELLOW BELL PEPPERS

PREPARATION TIME: 1 HOUR
PREPARE A DAY AHEAD
SERVES: 6

3 tablespoons butter
4 large leeks (whites only), washed,
    drained, and sliced
1 small onion, sliced
4 medium potatoes, peeled and sliced
3 cups chicken stock
1 tablespoon fresh lemon juice
2 cups milk
3 cups heavy cream
Salt and freshly ground black pepper
    to taste
1 *each* medium red and yellow bell
    pepper, deveined and seeded,
    chopped
Hungarian paprika for garnish

Vichyssoise, despite its French name, was first served at the Ritz-Carlton in New York in the early 1900s. It was the creation of French Chef Louis Diat who named it after the city near his home, Vichy, in memory of the fat succulent leeks he harvested for his mother's potato and leek potage.

In a large saucepan, melt the butter and sauté the leeks and onion over low heat 10–15 minutes. Add the potatoes, stock, and lemon juice and simmer 45 minutes.

In a blender or food processor fitted with the steel blade, puree the vegetables and soup so that it retains some texture (do not overprocess). Turn the mixture into a large saucepan and stir in the milk and *1 cup cream*. Season to taste. Stir in the peppers and simmer 2 minutes. Next day, add the remaining cream. Keep cold until ready to serve. Serve garnished with the paprika.

CHILLED INDIAN POTATO SOUP

PREPARATION TIME: 20 MINUTES
SERVES: 6

4 large potatoes, peeled and diced
¼ cup butter
1 large onion, chopped
2 Anaheim chiles, deveined and
    seeded, chopped
1 tablespoon minced fresh ginger
1½ cups unsweetened coconut milk*
3 cups chicken stock
Salt and freshly ground black pepper
    to taste
¾ cup plain low-fat yogurt
1 tablespoon Dijon mustard
Fresh mint for garnish
2 dried ground hot chiles or cayenne
    powder to taste

This surprising soup from southern India is an interesting variation of our vichyssoise. The coconut adds a hint of sweetness and the chiles a memorable bite.

In a large saucepan, cook the potatoes with water to cover, about 20 minutes or until tender. Drain and mash. In a large saucepan, melt the butter and sauté the onion and Anaheim chiles until soft, about 10 minutes. Add the potatoes, ginger, and coconut milk. In a blender or food processor fitted with the steel blade, process the mixture in batches until smooth. Return to the saucepan and add the stock, salt, and pepper. Bring to a boil, while stirring. Remove from the heat and stir in the yogurt and mustard. Chill. Serve garnished with the mint, and pass ground chiles or cayenne powder on the side.

*Unsweetened coconut milk is available in the specialty or ethnic sections of most supermarkets. To substitute, use 1 cup whole milk and ½ cup unsweetened, shredded coconut. Taste will be slightly different, but interesting, none the less.

CURRIED RED PEPPER AND EGGPLANT SOUP

PREPARATION TIME: 1 HOUR
CHILLING TIME: 4 HOURS
SERVES: 6 TO 9

2 tablespoons butter
2 tablespoons olive oil
1 medium onion, chopped
1 tablespoon curry powder
1 tablespoon Hungarian paprika
3 medium red bell peppers, deveined
    and seeded, chopped
1 medium eggplant, peeled and cut
    into cubes
1 quart chicken stock
½ cup half-and-half
Salt and freshly ground black pepper
    to taste
Chopped red pepper and parsley
    for garnish

This smooth and creamy curry soup can be spiced up with a garnish of roasted and peeled, deveined and seeded, chopped chile peppers.

In a medium-size saucepan set over medium heat, melt the butter and oil and sauté the onion until soft. Add the curry powder and paprika and cook over low heat 2 minutes. Add the peppers, eggplant, and chicken stock and bring to a boil. Reduce the heat, cover, and simmer 45 minutes, or until vegetables are soft.

Transfer to a blender or food processor fitted with the steel blade and puree. Return the mixture to the saucepan. Add the half-and-half, salt, and pepper. Allow the soup to cool, then chill 4 hours before serving. Garnish with the red pepper and parsley.

TOMATO, PEPPER, AND YOGURT SOUP

PREPARATION TIME: 10 MINUTES
CHILLING TIME: 30 MINUTES
SERVES: 6

2 pounds tomatoes, peeled, seeded,
  and chopped
2 medium red bell peppers, deveined
  and seeded, chopped
2 cups plain low-fat yogurt
1 clove garlic, minced
2 tablespoons freshly chopped herbs
  (basil, tarragon, or parsley, alone
  or in combination)
¼ cup fresh lemon juice
Salt and freshly ground black pepper
  to taste
Plain low-fat yogurt and freshly
  chopped herbs for garnish

This quick and simple recipe is easy on the cook when it's too hot for anyone to be in the kitchen. Follow with a big main-course salad.

In a blender or food processor fitted with the steel blade, puree the tomatoes and peppers. Add the next four remaining ingredients and combine until smooth. Salt and pepper to taste. Chill. Serve garnished with the yogurt and herbs.

SHELIA'S PUMPKIN
AND ROASTED RED PEPPER SOUP

PREPARATION TIME: 20 MINUTES
SERVES: 6

4 tablespoons butter
1 medium onion, chopped
2 tablespoons all-purpose flour
4 cups chicken stock
3 cups pumpkin puree*
1 *each* medium red and yellow bell
  pepper, roasted and peeled (page
  10), deveined and seeded,
  chopped
½ teaspoon ground nutmeg
½ teaspoon ground allspice
¾ cup half-and-half
Chopped red and yellow bell pepper
  for garnish

In a large saucepan, melt the butter and sauté the onion until soft. Sprinkle the mixture with the flour and cook 2–3 minutes. Gradually add the chicken stock, stirring until thick and smooth. Add the pumpkin, peppers, seasonings, and half-and-half. Stir the soup to warm through without boiling. Serve garnished with the chopped pepper.

---

*For 3 cups pumpkin puree, cut up 2½–3 pounds pumpkin and place in a large saucepan with water to cover. Cook about 10–15 minutes or until soft when pierced with a fork. Remove the skin and place the flesh in a blender or food processor fitted with the steel blade. Puree. Other varieties of winter squash like acorn, butternut, banana, and hubbard may be substituted (alone or in combination) for the pumpkin.

CREAM OF PEPPER, TOMATO, AND FENNEL SOUP

PREPARATION TIME: 1 HOUR 30 MINUTES
SERVES: 6

1 large fennel bulb, ends trimmed;
    reserve green fronds for garnish*
3 large onions, chopped
2 cups chicken stock
½ cup red wine
2 teaspoons freshly minced thyme, or
    ½ teaspoon dried
4 medium red bell peppers, deveined
    and seeded, chopped
3 medium tomatoes, chopped
1 cup heavy cream
Salt and freshly ground black pepper
    to taste
1 medium yellow bell pepper
    deveined and seeded, chopped
Chopped yellow or red bell pepper for
    garnish

Fennel is a pale green celery-like bulb with long, darker green fronds. It has a mild licorice taste and a juicy crunch.

Remove the outer layers from the fennel bulb and coarsely chop. In a large saucepan, set over low heat, cook the fennel, onions, *¼ cup stock*, wine, and thyme, covered, until onions are soft, about 15 minutes. Increase the heat to medium and add the remaining stock, peppers, and tomatoes. Cover and cook 1 hour, stirring occasionally.

In a blender or food processor fitted with the steel blade, puree the mixture in batches. Strain through a fine sieve, pressing with the back of a spoon. Return to the saucepan, whisk in the cream and bring to a boil for 5 minutes. Salt and pepper to taste. Stir in the yellow pepper. Garnish with the fennel fronds and chopped pepper.

*If fennel is not available, substitute equal amount of celery and 2 teaspoons fennel seeds.

MEXICAN TORTILLA SOUP
(SOPA DE TORTILLA)

PREPARATION TIME: 15 MINUTES
SERVES: 6

3 pasilla chiles, deveined and
   seeded, chopped
4 tablespoons vegetable oil
2 medium tomatoes, chopped
1 small onion, chopped
1 clove garlic, minced
6 cups chicken stock
1 cup tortilla chips
¼ cup freshly chopped cilantro
¼ cup grated cheddar cheese

This light and spicy soup is one of the most popular in Mexico. It is delicious and simple and makes for a zesty start to a grilled Mexican dinner.

In a large saucepan set over high heat, heat the oil and fry the chiles. Remove the chiles from the oil and set to drain on paper towels. Lower the heat to medium and add the tomatoes, onion, and garlic to the saucepan and cook, stirring frequently until it is a smooth sauce, about 10–15 minutes. Add the stock and bring to a boil. Add the tortilla chips and cilantro and cook about 3 minutes more. Serve each portion topped with the cheese and fried chiles.

AFRICAN PEANUT SOUP

PREPARATION TIME: 20 MINUTES
SERVES: 6

2 teaspoons cornstarch
3 cups milk
3 cups chicken stock
2 cups crunchy peanut butter
2 tablespoons grated onions
1 medium red bell pepper, chopped
Salt and freshly ground black pepper
   to taste
¼ - ½ teaspoon cayenne powder
   to taste
Fresh parsley and chopped red bell
   pepper for garnish

Many of today's favorite southern dishes were inspired by the Black slaves who adapted the recipes from their homeland to American ingredients. In Africa, this soup is made with ground nuts, a close relative of our peanuts. It is the original version of the classic Southern Peanut Soup.

In a small bowl, combine the cornstarch and milk until smooth. Pour the mixture into a large saucepan and add the remaining ingredients except garnish. Bring the soup to a boil and stir constantly. Lower the heat and simmer, uncovered, 15 minutes, continuing to stir. Serve the soup hot, garnished with the parsley and chopped pepper.

PREPARATION TIME: 20 MINUTES
SERVES: 6

2 medium potatoes, pared and diced
3 tablespoons butter
1 cup chopped onions
3 tablespoons all-purpose flour
3 cups milk
3 *each* medium green and red bell
   peppers, deveined and seeded,
   diced
2 cups grated cheddar cheese
Fresh parsley and chopped bell
   peppers for garnish

This lusty soup can be turned into a warming entrée with the addition of 1–2 cups cooked diced ham.

In a medium-size saucepan, cook the potatoes with enough water to cover, about 10 minutes or until tender. Drain, reserving ½ cup liquid. In a large saucepan, melt the butter and sauté the onions over moderate heat until tender. Blend in the flour and cook, stirring 2–3 minutes. Add the reserved potato water and milk to the onion mixture. Bring to a boil over high heat, stirring constantly. Reduce the heat to simmer, add the cooked potatoes and peppers and cook 5 minutes. Add the cheese and stir until the cheese melts, cooking an additional 5 minutes. Serve garnished with the parsley and chopped peppers.

HUNGARIAN GOULASH

PREPARATION TIME: 30 MINUTES
SERVES: 8 TO 10

3 tablespoons corn oil
2 medium onions, chopped
1 medium green bell pepper, chopped
1 clove garlic, crushed
5 cups water
1½ pounds beef stew meat, cut into
   1-inch cubes
3 tablespoons Hungarian paprika
2 teaspoons salt
½ teaspoon crushed red pepper, or
   to taste
1 teaspoon caraway seeds
2 pounds potatoes, peeled and cut
   into 1-inch cubes
One 16-ounce can crushed tomatoes,
   drained
12 cups cooked buttered noodles

This hearty dish is the Americanization of Hungarian gulyas, meaning shepherd's dinner. It makes a great supper for a crowd and leftovers freeze well.

In a 5-quart saucepan set over medium heat, heat the oil and sauté the onion, pepper, and garlic until tender. Add the water, beef, paprika, salt, red pepper, and caraway seeds and bring to a boil. Reduce the heat, cover, and simmer 2 hours, or until the meat is tender. Add the potatoes, cover, and cook 15 minutes, or until the potatoes are tender. Add the tomatoes. Cook the mixture until heated through. Serve over the noodles.

ITALIAN PEPPER AND SAUSAGE SOUP

PREPARATION TIME: 1 HOUR 30 MINUTES
SERVES: 8

2 pounds Italian sausage, parboiled
   and sliced
1 tablespoon olive oil
1 medium onion, chopped
2 cloves garlic, minced
2 Italian frying peppers, deveined and
   seeded, chopped
2 stalks celery, chopped
One 28-ounce can whole tomatoes
7 cups beef stock
1 teaspoon sugar
Salt and freshly ground black pepper
   to taste
3 cups diced red and green bell
   peppers
1 cup cooked noodles
½ cup grated Parmesan cheese
   for garnish

This makes a hearty supper soup served with plenty of crusty Italian bread and thick wedges of cheese.

In a large saucepan, brown the sausage and drain. Add the oil and sauté the onion, garlic, Italian peppers, and celery until soft. Add the tomatoes, stock, and sugar. Bring to a boil, then lower the heat and cover. Simmer about 1 hour. Add the peppers and cook 10 minutes. Stir in the cooked noodles and heat through. Serve sprinkled with the cheese.

CORN AND CHILE CHOWDER

PREPARATION TIME: 1 HOUR
SERVES: 6

3½ cups milk
1 medium onion, diced
1 bay leaf
¼ cup freshly chopped parsley
2 teaspoons freshly chopped thyme,
  or ½ teaspoon dried
3 teaspoons freshly chopped oregano,
  or 1 teaspoon dried
1 tablespoon whole peppercorns
3 cups whole kernel corn
1 cup water
2 tablespoons butter
4 Anaheim chiles, roasted and peeled
  (see page 10), deveined and seeded
1 large red or green bell pepper,
  deveined and seeded, chopped
Salt and freshly ground black pepper
  to taste
½ cup freshly shredded cheddar cheese
  for garnish
Fresh parsley for garnish

This hearty chowder makes a super supper with the addition of 1-2 cups cooked diced chicken or turkey. Serve with plenty of Roasted Pepper and Cheese Bread (see page 144).

In a medium-size saucepan over low heat, combine the milk, ½ the onion, bay leaf, parsley, thyme, oregano, and peppercorns. Bring to a boil, then remove from the heat and allow the herbs to steep 5 minutes. Strain.

In a blender or food processor fitted with the steel blade, puree 2 cups corn with 1 cup water in batches. Strain through a sieve using the back of a spoon. Set aside.

In a large saucepan set over low heat, melt the butter and sauté the remaining onion until soft. Add the remaining 1 cup corn and Anaheim chiles. Cook 3 minutes, then add pureed corn, strained milk, and bell pepper. Cook over low heat about 30 minutes, stirring frequently. Salt and pepper to taste. Serve the soup garnished with the cheese and parsley.

HOT AND SPICY RED PEPPER AND CABBAGE SOUP

PREPARATION TIME: 1 HOUR 15 MINUTES
SERVES: 6 TO 8

1-2 Anaheim or ancho chiles,
   deveined and seeded
3 tablespoons olive oil
½ teaspoon *each* dried savory,
   marjoram, and thyme
2 bay leaves
4 whole cloves
4 cloves garlic, minced
2 medium onions, sliced
4 medium red bell peppers, deveined
   and seeded, sliced
1 pound tomatoes, peeled, seeded,
   and chopped; juice reserved
6 cups water
1 cup shredded red or green cabbage
Salt and freshly ground black pepper
   to taste
Fresh parsley for garnish

To turn this spicy potage into a supper soup, add 1 pound cooked and crumbled lean ground beef and top each serving with shredded cheddar cheese.

In a small saucepan, place the chiles with enough water just to cover and bring to a boil. Simmer 20 minutes, then transfer to a blender or food processor fitted with the steel blade and puree. Turn into a small bowl and reserve.

In a large saucepan, warm the oil with the herbs, bay leaves, and cloves. Add the garlic and cook 30 seconds, then stir in the onions and peppers so that the vegetables are coated with the oil. Cover and cook over low heat about 5 minutes. If the vegetables are sticking, add ¼ cup water and cook another 5 minutes. Add the tomatoes, chile puree, and the water. Bring to a boil, then lower to simmer. Add the cabbage and cover with the liquid and cook on low 40 minutes.

In a blender or food processor fitted with the steel blade, puree the soup mixture in batches. Return to the saucepan, warm and season with the salt and pepper. Serve garnished with the parsley.

ENTRÉES AND MAIN COURSE FARE

AS A 10-YEAR-OLD, Mom's stuffed peppers were
my dinner favorite and a frequent request. The
fragrance of sausage and onions warmed our autumn
kitchen afternoons. And I loved eating the "dish"—
each round, plump pepper a perfect little dinner,
wearing its hat.

Just recently at the Fog City Diner in San Francisco,
my sister and I shared a grilled Anaheim chile stuffed
with Monterey Jack, fontina, and the local chèvre — a
house specialty. This aromatic pepper was served
complete with its hat on a small white plate. Sue and I
lapped up the last stringy bites of cheese with spicy
blue corn bread.

Here is a mélange of pepper entrées,
some stuffed and some not, that explore the vibrant
colors and flavors and give peppers their due.

MOM'S STUFFED PEPPERS

PREPARATION TIME: 20 MINUTES
BAKING TIME: 40 MINUTES
SERVES: 4

½ pound lean ground beef
½ pound mild Italian bulk sausage
1 tablespoon olive oil
1 small onion, diced
2 stalks celery, diced
4 large tomatoes, chopped
1 clove garlic, crushed
Salt and freshly ground black pepper
   to taste
½ cup fresh bread crumbs
2 tablespoons freshly chopped basil,
   or 2 teaspoons dried
1 tablespoon freshly chopped
   oregano, or 1 teaspoon dried
¼ cup freshly grated Parmesan cheese
4 large green bell peppers, tops
   removed and reserved, deveined
   and seeded

This may be prepared ahead and reheated the next day.

Preheat oven to 350°F. In a large heavy skillet, sauté the ground beef with the sausage until no longer pink. Drain. Transfer to a large bowl. Add the oil to the skillet and sauté the onion and celery. Add the onion mixture to the bowl containing the cooked meat.

Add the tomatoes and garlic to the skillet and simmer on low 10 minutes, stirring occasionally. Salt and pepper to taste. Reserve.

Add the bread crumbs, herbs, and cheese to the meat mixture and combine. Add *half of the tomato mixture* and blend well. Spoon the mixture into the green peppers. Stand the peppers upright in a lightly greased casserole. Spoon the remaining tomato mixture over the peppers and replace the tops on the peppers. Bake 40 minutes, or until the peppers are tender.

MEXICAN STUFFED CHILES
(CHILES RELLENOS)

PREPARATION TIME: 20 MINUTES
SERVES: 4

1 medium onion, chopped
2 cloves garlic, minced
1 tablespoon peanut oil
½ pound lean ground beef
   (or mixture of pork and beef)
½ cup chopped tomatoes
Salt and freshly ground black pepper
   to taste
¼ cup blanched chopped almonds
¼ cup raisins
4 Anaheim chiles
Flour for coating
2 eggs, separated
Peanut oil for frying
Red Hot Salsa Cruda or *Green Salsa*
   (see pages 126 and 127)

This is a classic, homey Mexican dish served a variety of ways throughout the country.

In a medium-size skillet, sauté the onion and garlic in the oil until transparent. Crumble the meat into the skillet and cook until no longer pink. Add the tomatoes, salt, pepper, almonds, and raisins. Simmer the mixture approximately 5 minutes.

Slit the chiles from top to tail, but leave whole. Devein and seed. Stuff the chiles with the meat mixture, then roll in the flour. In a small bowl, beat the egg yolks until light lemon-colored. In a small bowl, beat the egg whites until stiff, then slowly add the egg yolks. Pour at least ¾-inch oil into a heavy skillet and heat to smoke point (350°–400°F.). Dip the chiles in the egg mixture, then fry until golden on all sides, about 5–7 minutes. Drain on paper towels. Serve warm with the *Salsa*.

ITALIAN STUFFED PEPPERS
(PEPERONI IMBOTTITI)

PREPARATION TIME: 15 MINUTES
BAKING TIME: 30 MINUTES
SERVES: 6

¼ pound mild Italian bulk sausage
¼ pound lean ground beef
1 small onion, minced
1 clove garlic, minced
One 10-ounce package frozen
    spinach
½ cup dry bread crumbs
¼ cup freshly grated Romano cheese
½ cup freshly grated Parmesan cheese
1 egg
Salt and freshly ground black pepper
    to taste
8 large Italian green or bell peppers,
    deveined and seeded, but left whole
Olive oil

Bell peppers are a little bigger and wider than Italian. Add a few additional Italian peppers if you think some diners will have hearty appetites.

Preheat oven to 375°F. In a medium-size skillet, sauté the sausage and ground beef until no longer pink. Transfer to a large bowl with a slotted spoon. Sauté the onion and garlic in the skillet until transparent and transfer to the same bowl with a slotted spoon. Add the spinach, bread crumbs, cheeses, and egg with a dash of salt and pepper. Mix well. Fill the peppers with the mixture and arrange in a large greased casserole. Drizzle the peppers with the oil. Sprinkle with additional salt and pepper if desired. Bake 35 minutes, or until the peppers are tender.

TURKISH STUFFED PEPPERS

PREPARATION TIME: 45 MINUTES
SERVES: 4

½ pound ground lamb
½ cup canned tomatoes, drained;
    juice reserved
3 tablespoons ketchup*
1 small green bell pepper, deveined
    and seeded, minced
1 teaspoon salt
½ teaspoon cayenne powder
1 teaspoon dried oregano
2 tablespoons fresh lemon juice
1 teaspoon ground cumin
½ cup bulgur
4 medium red bell peppers, deveined
    and seeded, but left whole
1 cup beef stock
Yogurt for garnish
Fresh mint for garnish

Bulgur is a staple grain in the Middle East. It has a fine nutty taste and is highly nutritious. It is often confused with cracked wheat because the tastes are similar, though the process in producing them is somewhat different. Raw kernels of whole wheat that are crushed to varying degrees of fineness are called "cracked wheat." Whole wheat kernels that are first steamed, dried, then crushed are called "bulgur."

In a small bowl, mix together the lamb, tomatoes, ketchup, minced bell pepper, salt, cayenne powder, oregano, lemon juice, cumin, and bulgur. Stuff the whole peppers with the mixture and arrange side by side in a casserole or Dutch oven.

In a small saucepan, combine ½ cup reserved juice from the canned tomatoes and stock. Bring to a boil for 3 minutes. Pour the stock mixture over the peppers. Bring the casserole to a boil over medium heat. Cover with a plate that presses down on the peppers. Lower the heat and simmer 30 minutes, or until bulgur is cooked. Serve each pepper with a dollop of yogurt and the mint.

*The original version of this classic Turkish recipe calls for a homemade tomato paste, similar to ketchup.

PREPARATION TIME: 25 MINUTES
SERVES: 4

Juice of 2 limes
2 teaspoons lime zest
1 clove garlic, minced
2 chicken breast halves
Vegetable oil
Salt and freshly ground black pepper
   to taste
4 ounces Monterey Jack cheese,
   shredded
4 tablespoons white wine
4 large Anaheim or ancho chiles, slit,
   deveined and seeded, but left whole
Sour cream for garnish
Red Hot Salsa Cruda (see page 126)

This is a great summer entrée that can be made a day ahead. Stuff the chiles, cover with plastic wrap, and keep in the refrigerator. Grill just before serving.

Prepare the grill for medium flame. In a large baking dish, combine the lime juice, zest, and garlic. Place the chicken in the lime mixture and turn to coat thoroughly. Grill the chicken breasts brushing both sides with the oil until cooked and tender, about 15–20 minutes. Remove from the grill, remove the skin and bones, and shred the meat.

In a small bowl, combine the chicken with the cheese and wine. Stuff the chiles with the chicken mixture. Return the stuffed peppers to the grill and cook until all sides are charred, being careful not to lose too much stuffing. Remove. Serve with the sour cream and *Red Hot Salsa Cruda* on the side.

OLD-FASHIONED TEX-MEX CHILE

PREPARATION TIME: 2 HOURS 30 MINUTES
SERVES: 6 TO 8

2 pounds boneless pork shoulder, fat
    removed and reserved, cut into
    cubes
Flour for dredging
Salt and freshly ground black pepper to
    taste
2 tablespoons vegetable oil
3 medium onions, chopped
4 cloves garlic, minced
1 Anaheim chile, deveined and
    seeded, chopped
1 jalapeño pepper, deveined and
    seeded, chopped
1 *each* medium green and red bell
    pepper, deveined and seeded,
    chopped
1 tablespoon sugar
1 teaspoon chile powder

(continued)

Chile con carne is a Spanish-American term meaning "chile pepper with meat." The dish originated in Texas where it's nick-named "a bowl of red." Every year enthusiasts gather at the famous Annual World Championship Chile Cookoff in Terlingua, Texas, sponsored by the Chile Appreciation Society International, held the first Saturday of November. Although the hotness of chile is a virtue, it is the blend of flavors that determines the winner.

New Mexicans may use lamb instead of beef in their chile while many northern versions contain red kidney beans (an ingredient Texas purists shun).

In a large, heavy stew pot or Dutch oven set over medium heat, melt the pork fat. Dredge the pork cubes in the flour seasoned with the salt and pepper. Add the cubes to the pot, a few at a time, and brown. Remove the meat and set aside. Add the oil to the pot and sauté the onions and garlic until onions are transparent. Add the chiles and bell peppers and cook until soft.

In a small bowl, mix together the sugar, chile powder, cayenne powder, cumin, cinnamon, oregano, cilantro, and

(continued)

½ teaspoon cayenne powder
1 teaspoon ground cumin
½ teaspoon ground cinnamon
2 teaspoons dried oregano
¼ cup freshly chopped cilantro
1 tablespoon corn flour or white flour
Two 16-ounce cans whole tomatoes,
   undrained
One 6-ounce can tomato paste
3 cups beef stock
Grated cheddar and Monterey
   Jack cheese for garnish
Sour cream for garnish
Fresh cilantro for garnish

flour. Return the meat to the pot. Sprinkle the spice mixture over the meat and reduce heat to low. Stir in the tomatoes with liquid, tomato paste, and stock. Raise the heat and bring to a boil, then reduce heat to low and simmer 1–2 hours. Serve garnished with the cheeses, sour cream, and cilantro.

Those with a true passion for the piquant may want to increase the amount of fresh chiles and chile powder — and those with tastes more timid may want to skip the jalapeño.

FIERY TURKEY CHILE

PREPARATION TIME: 30 MINUTES
SERVES: 6

6 tablespoons olive oil
1 large onion, chopped
4 cloves garlic, minced
2 *each* medium red, green, and
   yellow bell peppers, deveined and
   seeded, diced
3–5 jalapeño peppers, deveined
   and seeded, diced (according to taste)
2 teaspoons chile powder
2 teaspoons ground coriander
1 teaspoon ground cumin
1 teaspoon ground cinnamon
1½ pounds turkey breast tenderloins,
   cut into cubes
Two 16-ounce cans tomato puree
1 cup beer
¼ cup grated unsweetened chocolate
Salt and freshly ground black pepper
   to taste
Sour cream for garnish
Grated cheddar cheese for garnish
Sliced avocado for garnish

In the Southwest and Mexico, chile powder is a blend of individual dried ancho, mulato, and pasilla chiles. Most commercial chile powders contain additional ingredients, diluting the punch of the dried chiles. If using a commercial powder, you can be a little heavy-handed. If you are using an expensive blend from a Mexican specialty store, beware. There may be more heat in the shake of your wrist than you expect. The best way to test the thermometer of chile powder is to sprinkle some on cottage cheese and taste.

In a large, heavy stew pot or Dutch oven, heat *3 tablespoons oil* over medium heat and sauté the garlic and onion 5 minutes. Add the bell and jalapeño peppers and sauté 10 minutes. Stir in the chile powder, coriander, cumin, and cinnamon and cook 5 minutes more. Remove from the heat and set aside.

In a large skillet, heat the remaining oil and brown the turkey in batches until cooked and no longer pink. Add the turkey, tomato puree, and beer to the pot and stir. Set over low heat, cover, and simmer 15 minutes, stirring occasionally. Add the chocolate, salt, and pepper. Serve immediately, passing the sour cream, cheese, and avocado separately.

VEGETARIAN CHILE

PREPARATION TIME: 1 HOUR 30 MINUTES
SERVES: 8

1 medium eggplant, cut into cubes
1 tablespoon salt
¼ cup olive oil plus ½ cup vegetable oil, combined
2 medium onions, diced
5 cloves garlic, minced
2 *each* medium red and green bell peppers, deveined and seeded, chopped
1 jalapeño pepper, deveined and seeded, chopped
One 35-ounce can Italian plum tomatoes
One 16-ounce can tomato puree
1 tablespoon chile powder, or to taste
1 tablespoon ground cumin
2 teaspoons dried oregano
2 teaspoons dried basil
2 teaspoons fennel seeds

(continued)

Sprinkle the eggplant with the salt in a large strainer or colander and allow to stand 1 hour, then pat dry with paper towels. In a large skillet set over medium heat, add *half the oil* and sauté the eggplant until tender. Turn into a large stock pot or Dutch oven.

In the same skillet, heat the remaining oil over medium-low heat and sauté the onions, garlic, bell and jalapeño peppers about 10 minutes or until soft. Add the onion mixture to the pot and place the pot over low heat. Add the tomatoes, chile powder, cumin, oregano, basil, fennel, parsley, salt, and pepper. Simmer, uncovered, stirring frequently for 30 minutes. Add the kidney beans, garbanzo beans, cilantro, and lime juice and continue to cook, stirring another 15 minutes. Serve over the rice, garnished with the cheese.

1 cup freshly chopped parsley
Salt and freshly ground black pepper
   to taste
1 cup canned and drained red
   kidney beans
1 cup canned and drained garbanzo
   beans
½ cup freshly chopped cilantro
1 tablespoon fresh lime juice
Cooked rice
Shredded Monterey Jack or cheddar
   cheese for garnish

SRI LANKA CURRY

PREPARATION TIME: 45 MINUTES
SERVES: 6

2 tablespoons vegetable oil
1 pound lean ground beef
2 medium onions, chopped
1 *each* medium red and green bell
    pepper, deveined and seeded,
    chopped
2½ cups water
½ cup unsweetened shredded coconut
2 tablespoons tomato paste
2 tablespoons shredded fresh ginger
2 whole sticks cinnamon
2 whole cloves
2 teaspoons curry powder
2 teaspoons chile powder
1 teaspoon ground turmeric
1 teaspoon ground cardamom
3 cups steamed white rice
Fiery Indian Chutney for garnish
    (see page 139)

Cinnamon and coconut are the signature ingredients of Sri Lankan curries. Sri Lanka is the area formerly known as Ceylon.

In a large skillet, heat the oil and cook the ground beef, onions, and peppers together until the meat is brown. Drain. Stir in the remaining ingredients except the rice and chutney. Heat to a boil, then reduce the heat and simmer, uncovered, until the vegetables are tender and curry is thick, about 20–30 minutes. Serve over the rice with the chutney.

CHINESE STIR-FRIED GINGER BEEF

PREPARATION TIME: 20 MINUTES
SERVES: 6

2 tablespoons peanut oil
2 pounds lean beef, cut into thin slices
   and 2-inch long strips
6 cloves garlic, minced
2 tablespoons shredded fresh ginger
1 large onion, coarsely chopped
10 Yung Ko peppers, blanched,
   deveined and seeded, cut into strips*
1 *each* medium yellow and red bell
   pepper, deveined and
   seeded, chopped
2 tablespoons soy sauce
¼ cup beef stock
½ teaspoon Chinese 5-spice powder
Freshly ground black pepper to taste
1 teaspoon sugar
2 tablespoons dry sherry
1 pound fresh spinach, washed
   and shredded
2 teaspoons cornstarch mixed
   with 2 tablespoons beef stock
Steamed white rice

In Hong Kong, the fresh produce markets abound with beautifully woven baskets full of shiny, waxy green, and small, fiery red chiles. Yung Ko is a thin, dark green or deep red power-packed pepper used in a variety of hot Oriental dishes.

In a wok or large skillet, heat the oil and stir-fry the beef until brown on all sides. Remove and set aside. Add the garlic, ginger, onion, Yung Ko peppers, and bell peppers and stir-fry until the onion is transparent. Add the soy sauce, stock, 5-spice powder, pepper, sugar, and sherry and toss together. Return the beef to the wok and add the spinach. Stir-fry until the spinach is wilted. Add the cornstarch mixture and continue to stir until the sauce is glossy and thick. Serve with the rice.

*Two jalapeño peppers may be substituted for Yung Ko.

PIQUANT CREOLE BEEF AND GRITS

PREPARATION TIME: 40 MINUTES
SERVES: 4

4 small beef filets
¼ cup all-purpose flour
¼ teaspoon salt
½ teaspoon sugar
½ teaspoon freshly ground
    black pepper
1 teaspoon dried oregano
2 teaspoons Hungarian paprika
⅛ teaspoon cayenne powder
2 tablespoons vegetable oil
2 large onions, chopped
7 cloves garlic, minced
1 *each* medium red, yellow, and green
    bell pepper, deveined and seeded,
    chopped

(continued)

Trim the meat. In a small paper bag, combine the flour, salt, sugar, black pepper, herb, and spices. Add the filets, one at a time, and shake. Remove the filets and shake off the excess coating and lay on a flat surface. Using a wooden mallet, pound the meat lightly to incorporate the seasoned flour.

In a large skillet set over medium-high heat, add the oil and sauté the filets just until brown on both sides. Remove the meat and set aside. Add the onions and garlic to the skillet and sauté until transparent. Add the bell peppers and Anaheim chile and sauté 1–2 minutes. Add the tomatoes and continue cooking, stirring constantly until the mixture becomes thick. Add the stock, sage, and bay leaf. Bring to a boil, reduce the heat to simmer, and cook 20–30 minutes or until thick. Add

(continued)

1 Anaheim chile, deveined and
   seeded, chopped
3 medium tomatoes, chopped
2 cups beef stock
1 large freshly chopped sage leaf, or
   ¼ teaspoon dried
1 bay leaf
½ cup *each* freshly chopped parsley
   and cilantro
Salt and freshly ground black pepper
   to taste
Dried hot chiles, crushed, to taste
4 cups water
½ teaspoon salt
1 cup quick-cooking hominy grits, or
   long grain white rice
1 *each* medium yellow and red bell
   pepper, sliced into rings

the parsley, cilantro, salt, pepper, and crushed chiles and cook, stirring 2 minutes. Return the meat to the skillet, cover, and reduce the heat to low.

In a medium-size saucepan, bring the water to a boil and add the salt. Slowly stir in the grits. Cook, stirring until thick, about 5 minutes. Mound the grits on a platter and place filets around it. Pour the sauce overall. Garnish with the pepper rings.

CHINESE SPARERIBS AND PEPPERS

PREPARATION TIME: 1 HOUR 15 MINUTES
SERVES: 4

1½ pounds pork spareribs, cut into
    1-inch lengths
4 tablespoons peanut oil
3 tablespoons water
3 cloves garlic, minced
1 small dry hot chile, seeded and
    crumbled
2 medium green bell peppers,
    deveined and seeded, cut into
    squares
1 medium red bell pepper, deveined
    and seeded, cut into squares
¼ cup water
1 tablespoon soy sauce
Steamed white or stir-fried rice

This is a casual dish served as part of an informal meal with a variety of courses in China. There diners eat the spareribs with chopsticks. Those of us who are less coordinated better rely on fingers and a ready supply of napkins. For centuries, chiles have been used by Oriental herbalists to prevent digestive diseases.

Trim the fat from the ribs. In a wok or large skillet set over high heat, add *2 tablespoons oil.* When the oil is hot, add the ribs and stir-fry until lightly browned, about 4 minutes. Add the water, reduce the heat to low, cover, and cook, stirring occasionally, until ribs are tender when pierced with a knife, about 30 minutes. Remove the ribs from the wok and discard the drippings.

Add the remaining 2 tablespoons oil and set the wok over high heat. Add the garlic, dry hot chile, and bell peppers and stir-fry about 1 minute. Add the ribs, the water, and soy sauce. Cover and cook 2 minutes. Remove the cover and cook another 2 minutes, or until liquid is evaporated. Serve with the rice.

HAITIAN SWEET AND SPICY PORK

PREPARATION TIME: 2 HOURS
MARINATING TIME: OVERNIGHT
SERVES: 6

2 medium onions, minced
¾ cup fresh orange juice
2 tablespoons orange zest
¼ cup fresh lemon juice
1 tablespoon lemon zest
1 jalapeño pepper, deveined and
    seeded, chopped
2 cloves garlic, minced
Salt and freshly ground black pepper
    to taste
3 pounds pork shoulder, cut into cubes
¼ cup peanut oil
1 *each* medium red and green bell
    pepper, deveined and seeded,
    diced
Steamed white rice
Haitian Hot Sauce (see page 128)

This recipe for Groits de Porc *is a specialty in Port-au-Prince, Haiti. It combines the refreshing flavors of orange and lemon with a bit of chile.*

In a medium-size glass bowl, combine the onions, orange juice and zest, lemon juice and zest, jalapeño, garlic, salt, and pepper. Add the pork, cover, and marinate overnight in the refrigerator.

To prepare, turn the pork and marinade into a casserole and add water just to cover the meat. Cover the casserole and simmer over medium heat until the meat is tender, about 1 hour 30 minutes. Drain.

In a heavy skillet, heat the oil and sauté the pork until crunchy, remove, and keep warm. Add the peppers to the skillet and sauté until tender crisp. Serve the pork and peppers with the rice and *Haitian Hot Sauce* on the side.

ITALIAN PEPPERS AND SAUSAGE

PREPARATION TIME: 40 MINUTES
SERVES: 4 TO 8

1–1½ pounds mild Italian sausage
2 tablespoons olive oil
1 large onion, coarsely chopped
1 clove garlic, minced
2 *each* medium red, green, and
  yellow bell peppers, deveined and
  seeded, cut into strips
One 15-ounce can Italian tomatoes
  with liquid
2 tablespoons freshly chopped basil,
  or 2 teaspoons dried
1 tablespoon freshly chopped
  oregano, or 2 teaspoons dried
1 teaspoon sugar
¼ cup sliced black olives
Salt and freshly ground black pepper
  to taste
6–8 Italian hard rolls or buns
Grated Parmesan cheese for garnish

In a large skillet set over medium heat, cook the sausage until browned. Remove from the skillet and set aside. Add the oil, onion, garlic, and peppers to the drippings and cook, stirring, until vegetables are soft, about 15 minutes. Stir in the tomatoes with liquid and add the herbs and sugar. Return the sausages and continue cooking, uncovered for 15 minutes. Uncover, increase the heat to medium-high and cook, stirring occasionally, until the liquid is reduced by more than half. Add the olives, salt, and pepper. Serve on crusty Italian rolls, garnished with the cheese.

GRILLED CHICKEN PIRI PIRI

PREPARATION TIME: 15-20 MINUTES
MARINATING TIME: 3 HOURS
SERVES: 4

1 serrano chile, deveined and seeded
4 cloves garlic
1 cup peanut oil
⅓ cup fresh lemon juice
Salt and freshly ground black pepper
   to taste
1 small frying chicken, cut into
   serving pieces

Piri Piri is a traditional Mozambique marinade used to spice up simple dishes. Try this on turkey, beef, or shellfish.

In a blender or food processor fitted with the steel blade, puree the serrano chile and garlic with *½ cup oil*. Add the remaining oil, lemon juice, and a dash of salt and pepper and process just until blended. Place the chicken pieces in a shallow glass pan and cover with the marinade. Cover and refrigerate at least 3 hours or overnight, turning pieces occasionally.

Prepare the grill for medium heat. Remove the chicken and reserve the marinade. Place the chicken on the grill and cook for 20–25 minutes, turning and basting with the marinade. Chicken is cooked when brown, juices run clean, and skin is pricked with a knife.

PREPARATION TIME: 1 HOUR 30 MINUTES
SERVES: 4 TO 6

One 5–6 pound roasting chicken
Salt and freshly ground black pepper
   to taste
2 cloves garlic
1 medium onion, chopped
Several sprigs fresh rosemary,
   oregano, and thyme (alone or in
   combination)
¼ cup melted butter
¼ cup vegetable oil
1 clove garlic, mashed
½ cup dry red wine

(continued)

This deliciously smoky sauce also tastes great on grilled chicken, roast turkey, and fried chicken.

To Roast Chicken

Preheat oven to 425°F. Wash the chicken under cold water and pat dry. Sprinkle the chicken inside and out with the salt and pepper. Then place the garlic, onion, and herbs inside the cavity. Truss by tying wing tips to body and leg bones together with string. In a small bowl, combine the butter and oil. Lay the chicken on its side on a rack in a shallow roasting pan. Brush the top with the butter and oil.

Roast the chicken for 15 minutes, basting once or twice with the combination butter and oil. Turn to other side and baste, roast another 15 minutes. Place the chicken breast side up and roast, basting occasionally, for 15 minutes per pound, about 1 hour 15–25 minutes for a 5-pound bird. Internal temperature of the chicken should be 180°F. in meaty thigh, and juices should run clear when pricked. Tent the chicken with aluminum foil to keep warm while preparing sauce.

(continued)

1½ pounds tomatoes, coarsely
   chopped
1½ pounds yellow and red bell
   peppers, roasted and peeled (see
   page 10), deveined and seeded,
   cut into strips
2 teaspoons freshly chopped thyme, or
   ½ teaspoon dried
2 teaspoons freshly chopped oregano,
   or ½ teaspoon dried
Salt and freshly ground black pepper
   to taste

Sauce

In a large heavy skillet, pour the drippings from the chicken, heat to medium-high, and add the mashed garlic. Add the wine and boil until reduced by half. Add the tomatoes, cover, and reduce the heat to medium and cook until the tomatoes are soft, about 3 minutes. Uncover and boil until slightly thickened, stirring occasionally, about 5 minutes. Add the pepper strips and pepper juices plus the herbs, salt, and pepper.

To serve, spoon the sauce onto individual plates and then place pieces of the carved chicken over the sauce. Garnish plates with strips of pepper from the sauce and pass additional sauce on the side.

DORO WAT
(AFRICAN FIRE CHICKEN STEW)

PREPARATION TIME: 1 HOUR 30 MINUTES
SERVES: 4

2 cups water
Juice of 1 lemon
1 medium stewing chicken, cut
   into serving pieces
2 medium onions, chopped
1 *each* medium red and green bell
   pepper, deveined and seeded,
   chopped
2 cloves garlic, minced
3 tablespoons butter
6 tablespoons tomato paste
1 teaspoon ground cardamom
1 teaspoon cayenne powder
1 red Fresno pepper, deveined and
   seeded, chopped
1 tablespoon shredded fresh ginger
6 hard-cooked eggs, peeled and
   quartered

Ethiopians like hot stuff. Cooks guard the family secret of their fiery stews. Doro Wat is a traditional dish, fragrant with garlic, cardamom, ginger, and pepper.

Pour the water and lemon juice into a large stew pot and add the chicken. Cover and simmer 30 minutes. In a small skillet, sauté the onions, bell peppers, and garlic in the butter until soft. Add the onion mixture to the pot and heat to boiling. Add the tomato paste, spices, Fresno pepper, and ginger and stir. Simmer the stew over low heat until the chicken is tender, about 20 minutes. Add the eggs and continue cooking 10 minutes more. Serve the chicken on a platter, garnished with the eggs.

BELL PEPPER AND TURKEY STIR-FRY

PREPARATION TIME: 15 MINUTES
SERVES: 4

¼ cup all-purpose flour
¼ cup sesame seeds
Salt and freshly ground black pepper
    to taste
1 pound turkey cutlets, cut into
    ½-inch strips
3 tablespoons peanut oil
1 *each* medium red, yellow, and
    green bell peppers, deveined and
    seeded, cut into strips
¼ cup sherry
4 tablespoons shredded fresh ginger
2 tablespoons soy sauce
2 cloves garlic, minced
Salt and freshly ground black pepper
    to taste
3 cups cooked rice
Toasted sesame seeds for garnish

In a plastic bag, combine the flour, sesame seeds, salt, and pepper. Add the turkey and shake until coated.

In a wok or large skillet, heat *2 tablespoons oil* over medium-high heat. Add the turkey and cook until no longer pink, about 3 minutes. Remove. Add the remaining oil to the wok and toss in the peppers, stir-frying about 1 minute. Return the turkey to the wok and add the sherry, ginger, soy sauce, and garlic. Season with the salt and pepper. Cook another 3–5 minutes, or until the peppers are tender crisp and chicken is springy. Serve over the rice, garnished with the sesame seeds.

JAMBALAYA

PREPARATION TIME: 45 MINUTES
SERVES: 8 TO 10

½ cup butter
1 pound andouille or smoked sausage, sliced
½ pound smoked ham, diced
3 medium onions, chopped
6 scallions, chopped
2 medium green bell peppers, deveined and seeded, diced
1 medium red bell pepper, deveined and seeded, diced
5 cloves garlic, minced
½ teaspoon dried crushed hot chiles or cayenne powder, to taste
¼ cup all-purpose flour
5 medium tomatoes, chopped, or 2 cups canned and drained

(continued)

Jambalaya is a spicy potage, characteristic of Cajun cooking. Cajun ancestors were Frenchmen who settled Nova Scotia (then called Acadia) in the 1700s. When the English acquired Canada and Nova Scotia, the natives refused to trade allegiance and speak English and so were deported. They made Louisiana their new homeland and cultivated a tradition of hearty one-pot meals that marry native fish, crawfish, rabbit, and squirrel with rice and beans into myriad gumbos and stews.

In a large skillet or Dutch oven, melt the butter and sauté the sausage and ham until lightly browned. Add the onions, scallions, peppers, garlic, and dried chiles. Cook over medium heat until the vegetables are soft, about 8 minutes. Stir in the flour and cook, stirring, 1–2 minutes. Stir in the remaining ingredients except the shrimp. Bring to a boil, cover the skillet, lower the heat, and simmer 25 minutes, or until all the liquid is absorbed. Add the shrimp and cook until pink, about 5 minutes.

JAMBALAYA (continued)

1 bay leaf
2 teaspoons freshly chopped thyme, or
   1 teaspoon dried
Salt and freshly ground black pepper
   to taste
3 cups chicken stock
1 cup cooked diced chicken
2 cups uncooked long grain rice
2 pounds raw shrimp, peeled and
   deveined

SWEET PEPPERS AND SHRIMP WITH FETA ON PASTA

PREPARATION TIME: 30 MINUTES
SERVES: 6

2 quarts water
8 ounces pasta
3 tablespoons olive oil
3 *each* medium yellow and red bell
   peppers, deveined and seeded,
   chopped
1 small onion, chopped
3 cloves garlic, minced
2 medium tomatoes, chopped
1 pound cooked shrimp, peeled and
   deveined
4 tablespoons freshly chopped basil,
  or 3 teaspoons dried
Salt and freshly ground black pepper
  to taste
½ pound feta cheese, crumbled
Fresh basil for garnish

This pretty, colorful dish is terrific served hot or at room temperature. The feta adds a delicious salty complement to the sweet peppers.

In a large saucepan, bring the water to a rolling boil. Add the pasta and cook, uncovered, 10–12 minutes. Drain. In a large skillet set over medium heat, heat the oil and the peppers, onion, and garlic about 10 minutes. Add the tomatoes and cook, stirring occasionally, 5 minutes. Add the shrimp, basil, salt, and pepper.

Drain the pasta and serve the shrimp and peppers over the pasta. Sprinkle with the cheese. Garnish with the basil.

SANTA FE EGGS

PREPARATION TIME: 20 MINUTES
SERVES: 2

Vegetable oil for frying
2 blue or yellow corn tortillas
1 tablespoon butter
4 eggs
¼ cup freshly shredded Monterey Jack
 cheese
Red Hot Salsa Cruda (see page 126)
Fresh cilantro for garnish

Santa Fe's southwestern fare is classic northern New Mexican cuisine —pure, simple, and very, very good. It calls for blue corn tortillas, originally native to the Rio Grande area, and pure red chile sauce. The city hosts over 200 restaurants in a town of just over 50,000 people. One of the most popular spots is a nonassuming restaurant, The Shed, located near the cathedral in the oldest part of town, Prince Patio, dating back to 1692. Open only for breakfast and lunch, its Huevos a la Mexicana draws long lines for Sunday brunch.

In a large, heavy skillet, heat ½-inch oil over medium heat to very hot, but not smoking. Add 1 tortilla and cook until lightly toasted around the edges and beginning to blister, about 30 seconds. Drain on paper towels and keep warm. Repeat the process with the remaining tortilla.

Pour the oil from the skillet, add the butter and melt. Break the eggs into the skillet and cook until just set. Place the tortillas on separate plates and top each with the 2 eggs, cheese, and a spoonful of *Red Hot Salsa Cruda*. Serve garnished with the cilantro and pass additional salsa separately.

PREPARATION TIME: 20 MINUTES
SERVES: 8

8 slices bacon, cut into small pieces
2 *each* medium red, green, and
    yellow bell peppers, deveined and
    seeded, chopped
2 cups coarsely chopped cooked ham
½ cup freshly chopped parsley
16 eggs
¼ cup milk
Salt and freshly ground black pepper
    to taste

This colorful Basque inspired omelette makes a quick and easy supper and elegant brunch dish. Serve with Corny Red Pepper Corn Bread (see page 142).

In a large skillet set over medium-low heat, cook the bacon until crisp. Remove with a slotted spoon and set aside. Raise the heat and sauté the peppers in the pan drippings until tender crisp. Stir in the ham and parsley. Cook until heated through. Remove the mixture with a slotted spoon and set aside. Keep warm.

In a large bowl, combine the eggs, milk, salt, and pepper. Pour into the skillet, return the heat to low, and cook the eggs, gently lifting cooked area so that uncooked area may flow underneath. When the eggs are cooked (set but not rubbery), distribute the peppers, ham, and bacon over the surface. Remove from the skillet and serve hot.

MAC AND CHEESE . . . CHA CHA CHA

PREPARATION TIME: 45 MINUTES
SERVES: 6

2 tablespoons olive oil
1 small jalapeño pepper, deveined
  and seeded, chopped
1 *each* medium red and green bell
  pepper, deveined and seeded,
  chopped
3 cups cooked elbow macaroni
3 tablespoons butter
2 tablespoons all-purpose flour
4 tablespoons milk
½ cup freshly grated Monterey Jack
  cheese
Salt and freshly ground black pepper
  to taste

When my son turned two, he refused to eat anything but macaroni and cheese. Somehow I always made more than I intended and found myself concocting ways to use up leftovers for my husband's supper later. This became a Friday night special.

Preheat oven to 350°F. Grease a medium-size baking dish or casserole. In a medium-size saucepan set over medium heat, add the oil and sauté the jalapeño and bell peppers until soft. Turn into a large bowl. Add the cooked macaroni and toss.

In a small saucepan, melt the butter and add the flour and milk, stirring constantly. Add most of the cheese and stir until melted. Pour the sauce over the macaroni and peppers and toss gently to combine thoroughly. Salt and pepper to taste. Turn the macaroni into the prepared casserole. Cover with the remaining cheese and bake until bubbly and hot, about 15 minutes.

PREPARATION TIME: 1 HOUR 15 MINUTES
SERVES: 4

4 extra large baking potatoes
3 tablespoons vegetable oil
½ medium red onion, chopped
1 clove garlic, minced
1 jalapeño pepper, deveined and
   seeded, chopped
1 medium red bell pepper, deveined
   and seeded, chopped
½ cup sour cream or sour half-and-half
¼ cup freshly grated Monterey Jack
   cheese
¼ cup freshly grated cheddar cheese
½ teaspoon ground cumin
Salt and freshly ground black pepper
   to taste
Shredded cheeses
Red Hot Salsa Cruda (see page 126)

These hearty stuffed potatoes make a nutritious meal in a peel. They can be made ahead and baked later.

Preheat oven to 400°F. Bake the potatoes 50–60 minutes or until soft when pierced with a knife. While the potatoes are baking, heat the oil in a medium-size skillet over medium heat. Add the onion, garlic, jalapeño, and bell pepper. Cook until the onion is transparent.

Lower the heat to 350°F. Slit the baked potatoes and scoop out the pulp, leaving ½-inch thick shell, and place the pulp in a medium-size bowl. Add the sour cream, cheeses, cumin, and sautéed onion and peppers. Stir to combine. Salt and pepper to taste.

Stuff the shells with the filling, mounding up to the top. (Bake leftover filling in a greased casserole.) Place the potatoes on an aluminum foil-lined baking sheet. Sprinkle with the additional cheese. Bake 20 minutes, or until the potatoes are hot and cheese is melted. Serve with *Red Hot Salsa Cruda* on the side.

ANGEL HAIR PASTA WITH BELL PEPPERS IN FRESH TOMATO SAUCE

PREPARATION TIME: 1 HOUR
SERVES: 8

¼ cup olive oil
¼ cup vegetable oil
1 medium onion, minced
6 cloves garlic, minced
3 pounds plum tomatoes, seeded and
 chopped
½ cup freshly chopped basil
Salt and freshly ground black pepper
 to taste
3 *each* medium red and yellow bell
 peppers, deveined and seeded,
 sliced
1½ pounds angel hair pasta (capellini)
1 tablespoon olive oil
¼ cup freshly grated Parmesan cheese
¼ cup freshly grated mozzarella
 cheese
Fresh basil for garnish

It's clear why capellini pasta is also called "angel hair." These delicate wisps of pasta are heavenly.

In a cup, combine the oils and set aside. In a large, heavy skillet set over low heat, add *half the oil* and sauté the onion and *3 cloves garlic* until transparent. Increase the heat and add the tomatoes, basil, salt, and pepper. Bring to a boil, then lower the heat and simmer, uncovered, until most of the liquid evaporates, stirring occasionally, about 20 minutes.

In another heavy skillet, heat the remaining oil and sauté the peppers with the remaining garlic until tender and the edges begin to brown, about 10 minutes. In a large pot of rapidly boiling water, add the pasta and 1 tablespoon vegetable oil. Cook until tender but al dente. Drain well. To serve, toss the pasta with the tomato sauce, peppers, and cheese, reserving some to arrange on top. Garnish with the basil.

PASTA WITH PANCETTA, TOMATOES, AND HOT PEPPERS

PREPARATION TIME: 45 MINUTES
SERVES: 6

¼ cup butter
4 tablespoons vegetable oil
1 medium onion, chopped
2 slices pancetta, cut into ½-inch strips
3 cups canned Italian tomatoes,
　broken up with spoon
1 small jalapeño pepper, deveined
　and seeded, chopped
1 *each* medium red and green bell
　pepper, deveined and seeded,
　chopped
Salt and freshly ground black pepper
　to taste
1 quart water
1 pound spiral or nugget pasta
　(rotini or radiatore)
½ cup freshly grated Parmesan cheese
2 tablespoons freshly grated Romano
　cheese

Pancetta is a nonsmoked traditional Italian bacon. It's available in Italian specialty shops or the butcher department of many large supermarkets. Sliced ham may be substituted.

In a large skillet over medium heat, melt the butter and oil and sauté the onion until transparent. Add the pancetta and sauté about 1 minute. Add the tomatoes, peppers, salt, and pepper. Cook over medium heat, stirring occasionally, about 25 minutes.

In a large pot, bring the water to a boil, add the pasta and cook 10 minutes, or until the pasta is al dente. Drain. Turn pasta into a warm serving bowl, add the sauce, and toss with the cheeses. Serve with additional cheese on the side.

AUTUMN PEPPER AND BEAN STEW

PREPARATION TIME: 2 HOURS
SERVES: 6

1 cup mixed dried beans (pinto, black,
   kidney, black beans), soaked
   overnight and drained*
4 tablespoons vegetable oil
1 medium onion, diced
2 cloves garlic
1 *each* medium red and green bell
   pepper, deveined and seeded,
   chopped
1 teaspoon ground cumin
1 teaspoon dried oregano
1 teaspoon ground cinnamon
4 whole cloves
1 tablespoon Hungarian paprika

(continued)

This is the sort of dish that gets better and better as it's reheated in succeeding days.

   Drain and sort the beans. Place in a large pot, cover with water, and cook about 1 hour 30 minutes or until tender.
   In a large skillet, heat the oil and sauté the onion, garlic, and bell peppers until tender. Add the spices, ½ *cup stock*, and tomatoes and cook 5 minutes. Add the squash with the remaining stock and continue cooking 30 minutes. When the squash is about half cooked but still firm, add the corn, beans, and jalapeño. Cook until the squash is tender, about 15–20 minutes. Salt and pepper to taste.

*In a hurry? Substitute one 16-ounce can pinto, kidney, or black beans.

2 cups chicken or vegetable stock
1 pound tomatoes (fresh or canned),
   chopped; juice reserved
2 cups winter squash (acorn, pumpkin,
   or hubbard), peeled and cut into
   1-inch cubes
1½ cups whole kernel corn
1 jalapeño pepper, deveined and
   seeded, chopped
Salt and freshly ground black pepper
   to taste

MEXICAN PIZZA

PREPARATION TIME: 30 MINUTES
SERVES: 10–12-INCH PIZZA

One 10–12-inch pizza dough
3 tablespoons olive oil
2 cloves garlic, minced
3 tablespoons *Dried Chile Paste* (see
    page 130)
1 medium red onion, finely chopped
¼ cup *each* freshly shredded
    Muenster, cheddar, and Monterey
    Jack cheese
1 Anaheim chile, deveined and
    seeded, chopped
1 *each* medium red and green bell
    pepper, deveined and seeded,
    chopped
1 medium tomato, chopped
Salt and freshly ground black pepper
    to taste
¼ cup freshly chopped cilantro

This makes an easy, light supper served with a big green salad. Or, take it along on a romantic picnic. Did you know that chiles have long been considered an aphrodisiac? In Mexican folklore, those who eat spicy foods and love hot stuff are pretty hot themselves.

Preheat oven to 500°F. Brush the pizza dough with *1 tablespoon oil* and sprinkle with the garlic. Spread with the *Dried Chile Paste* and sprinkle with the onion. Combine the cheeses and sprinkle *all but ¼ cup* on the pizza. In a small bowl, toss the Anaheim chile, bell peppers, and tomato with the remaining oil and spread over the pizza. Season with the salt and pepper. Sprinkle the remaining cheese over all. Bake 10 minutes, or until the crust is brown and cheese is bubbly. Garnish with the cilantro.

PREPARATION TIME: 45 MINUTES
SERVES: 6

6 Anaheim or ancho chiles, roasted
    and peeled (see page 10)
¼ cup butter
2 medium onions, chopped
½ cup heavy cream
½ cup sour cream
Salt and freshly ground black pepper
    to taste
1 cup vegetable oil
12 corn tortillas
4 ounces Monterey Jack cheese,
    shredded
6 ounces Muenster cheese, shredded
3 cups *Red Hot Salsa Cruda*
    (see page 126)
Shredded lettuce
Chopped tomatoes
Sour cream

In the early 1700s, physicians recommended hot peppers to "persuade" those with little appetite to become interested. This easy, spicy casserole is just what the doctor ordered for a dull winter's night.

Devein and seed the chiles and cut into strips. Preheat oven to 375°F. In a medium-size skillet set over medium heat, melt the butter and sauté the onions until light. Add the Anaheim chiles, heavy cream, and sour cream and simmer 3–4 minutes, stirring occasionally. Salt and pepper to taste.

In a large skillet, heat the oil to 300°F. Dip each tortilla in the hot oil, then drain on paper towels. In a small bowl, toss together the cheeses.

To fill the tortillas, spread each with 1–2 tablespoons *Red Hot Salsa Cruda*, then the chile pepper mixture, then 3–4 tablespoons cheese. Roll up and place seam side down in a shallow casserole or individual baking dishes. Pour the remaining *Salsa* over the top and sprinkle with the remaining cheese. Place in the oven until cheese is hot and bubbly, about 15 minutes. Serve topped with the lettuce, tomatoes, and sour cream.

CREOLE RED BEANS AND RICE

PREPARATION TIME: 2 HOURS 15 MINUTES
SERVES: 6

Beans

2 cups dried red or pinto beans (not
  kidney), soaked overnight, rinsed,
  drained, and sorted through*
1 large onion, sliced
6 cloves garlic, peeled
1 bay leaf
2 teaspoons pickling spice

Sauce

2 tablespoons bacon drippings or
  butter
1½ pounds pork butt or boneless
  shoulder, cut into strips

(continued)

Red Rice and Beans is a Creole classic, pairing protein and carbohydrate in a complete and tasty meal. Serve it with a big green salad and plenty of corn bread.

In a large pot, place the beans with the onion, garlic, bay leaf, and pickling spice and cover with water 4–5 inches above the beans. Bring to a boil, then reduce the heat to simmer. Cook until tender, about 1–1 hour 30 minutes. Remove the pot from the heat and set aside.

To make the sauce, melt the drippings in a large heavy saucepan or Dutch oven. Sauté the pork until brown. Add the onion and garlic and sauté until onion is soft. Add the tomatoes and stir, cooking an additional 2 minutes. Add all the remaining ingredients except rice. Bring to a boil, reduce heat, and simmer, stirring frequently, 2 hours. The sauce should be thick and rich.

To serve, arrange the rice in a ring around the outside of a large serving platter or shallow bowl. Pour the beans into the center. Sprinkle with the parsley.

---

*In a hurry, substitute two 16-ounce cans pinto beans; drain, and simply heat first with a little chopped garlic and onion.

1 large onion, chopped
5 cloves garlic, chopped
3 medium tomatoes, chopped
½ cup beef stock
2 jalapeño peppers, deveined and
  seeded, chopped
1 *each* medium red and green bell
  pepper, deveined and seeded,
  chopped
3 stalks celery, chopped
¼ pound okra, cut into rings
½ cup freshly minced parsley
1 teaspoon dried oregano
1 tablespoon chile powder
1 bay leaf
1 tablespoon sugar
¼ cup dry red wine
Salt and freshly ground black pepper
  to taste
4 cups cooked white rice
Fresh parsley for garnish

No ONE EVER HAD to tell me to eat my
grandmother's vegetables. In fact, I usually
accepted seconds of her succotash
(sweet white corn and pretty bits of red pepper).
Sometimes, she'd sauté onions and green
and red peppers as a side dish to meat loaf, but
I'd spoon it on top of my slice instead of
ketchup. Other times, farm-stand fresh
green and red bell peppers were stuffed
with leftover rice, or sliced and fried with
potatoes, or chopped and tossed
with fresh peas. Served alongside a simple
roast chicken or pan-fried fish,
peppers make meals special.

SAN FRANCISCO CHILES

PREPARATION TIME: 20 MINUTES
SERVES: 6

6 Anaheim chiles, roasted and peeled
  (see page 10)
One 3-ounce package cream cheese
¼ cup freshly shredded cheddar
  cheese
¼ cup freshly shredded Monterey Jack
  cheese
1 medium red bell pepper, deveined
  and seeded, diced

This recipe is quick and easy and very rich. Serve as an accompaniment to a light meal of grilled fish or poultry. The chiles can be roasted then reheated while the meat is grilling.

Slit the Anaheim chiles and remove the veins and seeds but leave chiles intact. In a small bowl, combine the cream cheese with the cheeses and bell pepper. Stuff the prepared chiles as full as possible. Place the stuffed chiles on aluminum foil and return to the grill or place in 375°F. oven and bake 10 minutes, or until the cheese is bubbly.

STIR-FRIED PEPPERS AND SNOW PEAS

PREPARATION TIME: 15 MINUTES
SERVES: 6

½ cup chicken stock
1 tablespoon cornstarch
2½ teaspoons soy sauce
½ teaspoon brown sugar
3 tablespoons peanut oil
1 teaspoon shredded fresh ginger
1 clove garlic, minced
1 *each* medium red and yellow bell
    pepper, deveined and seeded, cut
    into thin strips
½ pound fresh snow peas, tough
    ends and strings removed, or one
    10-ounce package frozen

This is a very bright and pretty addition to a simple dinner of grilled poultry or fish. Add a bit of cooked diced chicken or ground beef and serve over steamed rice for a light meal.

In a small bowl, combine the stock, cornstarch, soy sauce, and brown sugar. Set aside. In a wok or a large skillet, set over high heat, heat the oil. When the oil is hot, add the ginger and garlic and stir once. Add the vegetables and toss to coat. Stir-fry 1 minute. Add the stock mixture and cook, stirring until sauce bubbles and thickens, about 30 seconds. Serve immediately.

OKRA, TOMATOES, AND PEPPERS

1 pound fresh okra (or two 10-ounce
   packages frozen)
4 slices bacon
1 medium onion, chopped
3 medium tomatoes, chopped
1 medium green bell pepper,
   deveined and seeded, chopped
1 small jalapeño pepper, deveined
   and seeded, chopped
Salt and freshly ground black pepper
   to taste

This is a classic soul food vegetable dish to add fire to a plate of home-fried chicken.

If using fresh, wash the okra and remove the tops and tails. Dry on paper towels and reserve. In a large heavy skillet, cook the bacon until crisp and remove with a slotted spoon. Drain on paper towels, crumble, and reserve for garnish. Add the okra and onion to the bacon fat in the skillet and sauté until the onion is transparent. Add the tomatoes and peppers and simmer over low heat until the okra is tender, about 10 minutes. Salt and pepper to taste. Serve garnished with the bacon.

GRILLED ITALIAN PEPPERS AND GARLIC

PREPARATION TIME: 40 MINUTES
SERVES: 6 TO 8

2 *each* medium red, green, and
    yellow bell peppers, deveined and
    seeded, thinly sliced
2 Italian frying peppers, deveined
    and seeded, thinly sliced
6 cloves garlic, peeled
2 tablespoons vegetable oil
2 tablespoons olive oil
1 tablespoon freshly chopped
    oregano
2 tablespoons freshly chopped basil
Fresh basil for garnish

In the winter, try sautéing the vegetables and garlic in a large skillet set over low heat, stirring frequently. This delicious mild, garlicky combination makes a terrific filling for a pita sandwich topped with plenty of Parmesan and mozzarella cheese.

Prepare the grill for medium-low heat. Generously grease a 12-inch piece of aluminum foil. Spread the vegetables over the foil and drizzle with the oils and herbs. Place the foil on the grill and cook, stirring occasionally to prevent sticking. Add more oil if necessary. Cooking time will vary with the heat from 15–25 minutes. Vegetables are cooked when the garlic is a caramel color and the peppers are golden brown around the edges. Serve garnished with the basil.

GRILLED PEPPERS, EGGPLANT, AND RED ONION

PREPARATION TIME: 30 MINUTES
SERVES: 4

1 *each* medium red and green bell
  pepper, deveined and seeded,
  cut into 1-inch pieces
1 small eggplant, peeled and
  cut into 1-inch pieces
1 small red onion, peeled and
  cut into 1-inch pieces
2 cloves garlic, minced
2 tablespoons olive oil
2 tablespoons vegetable oil
Salt and freshly ground black pepper
  to taste
Fresh parsley for garnish

This easy summery dish makes a great accompaniment to fish and chicken. It holds well and may be prepared or started before the entrée is placed on the grill. In the winter, try broiling the vegetables. Follow the same recipe directions, but check vegetables more often and stir frequently.

Prepare the grill for medium-low heat. In a small bowl, toss the vegetables and garlic with the oils, salt, and pepper. Generously grease a 12-inch piece of aluminum foil, turned up at the edges to form a border. Spread the vegetables over the foil. Place on the grill and cover. Check, stirring the vegetables occasionally to keep from sticking. Sprinkle with the vegetable oil if necessary. Cooking time will vary between 20–30 minutes depending on the heat. Vegetables are done when the eggplant is soft and the peppers and onion are golden brown at the edges. May be served warm or cold, garnished with the parsley.

GREEK PEPPERS AND GARLIC

PREPARATION TIME: 1 HOUR 15 MINUTES
SERVES: 6

2 medium red bell peppers, deveined
　　and seeded, but left whole
6 small hot chiles (use a variety of red,
　　green, and yellow), deveined and
　　seeded, but left whole
2 Anaheim chiles, deveined and
　　seeded, but left whole
6 scallions
25 cloves garlic, peeled
1 medium onion, cut into thick rings
1 bunch dill, tied together
1 bunch parsley, tied together
Olive oil

This is a rich, fiery Greek dish often served with thick slices of hearty bread and lots of retsina.

In a large skillet with a tight-fitting lid, place all the vegetables in a single layer. Place the dill and parsley on the top. Add the oil to fill the skillet 1 inch deep. Place the skillet over low-medium heat. As soon as the oil begins to simmer, reduce the heat to the lowest setting and turn the vegetables once. Cover and cook 45 minutes to 1 hour, or until the scallions are soft. Remove from the heat and allow to cool, covered. Serve as an accompaniment to roast pork or chicken. Delicious spread on crusty bread.

MEXICAN CREAMED CORN

PREPARATION TIME: 15 MINUTES
BAKING TIME: 30 MINUTES
SERVES: 6

¼ cup butter
1 small onion, chopped
1 clove garlic, minced
5 Anaheim or poblano chiles, roasted
  and peeled (see page 10)
4 cups whole kernel corn
¼ pound mild cheddar cheese,
  shredded
Salt and freshly ground black pepper
  to taste
Sour cream for garnish

This rich side dish is a simplified version of the classic Mexican Elote Con Crema. Try leaving the chiles whole and stuffing them with the corn and cream mixture. Or, serve with warm tortillas and a big salad for a simple supper.

Preheat oven to 350°F. In a Dutch oven or flameproof casserole, melt the butter over medium heat and sauté the onion and garlic until soft. Devein and seed the Anaheim chiles and cut into strips. Add to the onions and cover. Cook 8 minutes. Add the corn, cheese, salt, and pepper to the Dutch oven. Cover, place in the oven, and bake 30 minutes. Serve with the sour cream on the side.

KENYAN CORN

PREPARATION TIME: 15 MINUTES
SERVES: 4

1 tablespoon butter
1 medium onion, chopped
1 clove garlic, minced
3 cups whole kernel corn
1 teaspoon cornstarch
¾ cup unsweetened coconut milk*
2 medium red bell peppers, deveined
   and seeded, chopped
¼ teaspoon curry powder
Salt and freshly ground black pepper
   to taste
2 tablespoons fresh lemon juice
¼ cup freshly chopped cilantro

According to a close college friend who served with the Peace Corps in Kenya, Swahili cuisine is an exotic blend of African, Arab, and Indian cultures. Even everyday side dishes assume vivid colors and flavors.

In a heavy skillet, melt the butter. Add the onion and garlic and sauté until golden. Add the corn. Combine the cornstarch with ½ cup coconut milk, stirring well. Add the cornstarch mixture to the corn mixture with the peppers, curry powder, salt, and pepper. Add the remaining coconut milk and lemon juice. Stir. Garnish with the cilantro.

*Unsweetened coconut milk is available at Indian specialty stores and in the ethnic section of most supermarkets.

RED PEPPER AND CORN PANCAKES

PREPARATION TIME: 45 MINUTES
SERVES: 8

2 cups whole kernel corn
1 egg yolk
¼ cup cornmeal
¼ cup all-purpose flour
2 teaspoons freshly chopped thyme, or
    ½ teaspoon dried
½ teaspoon salt
¼ teaspoon freshly ground black
    pepper
1 medium red bell pepper, deveined
    and seeded, chopped
4 egg whites
2 tablespoons olive oil

These light pancakes make a delicious side dish to Vegetarian Chile *(see page 60) or serve topped with sour cream and* Roasted Herbed Peppers *(see page 12) for a light entrée.*

In a large bowl, combine the corn, egg yolk, cornmeal, flour, thyme, salt, and pepper. Add the bell pepper and combine thoroughly.

In a separate bowl, whisk the egg whites until soft peaks form. Fold half of the egg whites into the corn mixture and blend well. Then carefully fold in the remaining egg whites. Do not over mix (it will not appear totally blended).

Heat a large heavy skillet over medium heat. Add a little of the oil to coat. When hot, drop the batter by tablespoons into the skillet. Do not let the edges touch. Cook until the bottom of each pancake is golden, about 3 minutes. Flip the pancakes and cook another 3 minutes. Remove finished pancakes from the skillet and keep warm. Repeat the process, coating the skillet with oil each time. Serve with *Red Hot Salsa Cruda* (see page 126) or *Chile Butter* (see page 130).

RED AND YELLOW PEPPERS WITH ARTICHOKES AND PASTA

PREPARATION TIME: 15 MINUTES
SERVES: 6

One 14-ounce can water-packed
    artichokes, drained and halved
1 tablespoon fresh lemon juice
4 tablespoons vegetable oil
1 *each* medium red and yellow bell
    pepper, deveined and seeded, cut
    into strips
1 clove garlic, minced
1 tablespoon freshly chopped
    oregano, or 2 teaspoons dried
1 pound fresh linguine
¼ cup freshly chopped parsley for
    garnish

This makes a very easy and very pretty side dish or first course. You may omit the pasta, double the other ingredients, and serve this as a vegetable side dish.

Toss the artichokes with the lemon juice and set aside. In a large heavy skillet set over medium heat, add the oil and sauté the artichokes, peppers, garlic, and oregano until the peppers are tender crisp, stirring frequently, about 10 minutes.

Bring a large pot of water to a rolling boil and cook the pasta 2–3 minutes (it should be firm). Drain. Arrange the pasta on a large serving platter and arrange the peppers and artichokes overall. Garnish with the parsley.

ROASTED PEPPER RISOTTO

1 *each* medium red and yellow bell
   pepper, roasted and peeled (see
   page 10)
4 cups chicken stock
3 tablespoons butter
2 tablespoons vegetable oil
1 small onion, finely chopped
1 clove garlic, minced
1 ½ cups uncooked Italian arborio rice
Up to 1 cup boiling water (as needed)
½ cup freshly grated Parmesan cheese
Salt and freshly ground black pepper
   to taste

Risotto refers to the Italian cooking method of preparing rice. (It is not a special type of rice itself.) In preparing risotto, the objective is to force the rice to absorb the hot stock until it swells, becoming at once firm and creamy. The process requires that the stock be added very slowly and the rice not drown in the liquid or boil —low, even heat is critical. If the liquid evaporates too quickly, the rice won't cook evenly and will be soft outside and chalky inside. If the heat is too low, the rice will become gluey.

Slice, devein, and seed the peppers. Cut into thin strips, reserving juices. Set aside.

In a large saucepan, bring the stock to a slow steady simmer. In a heavy casserole or large saucepan, melt *2 tablespoons butter* and all the oil over medium heat and sauté the onion and garlic until transparent. Add the rice and stir until well coated, sautéing lightly. Slowly add ½ cup simmering stock and stir while cooking until the rice absorbs the stock. When the rice

(continued)

begins to dry out, add another ½ cup stock, continuing to cook and stir to prevent the rice from sticking. Continue to add the stock as the rice absorbs it and begins to dry out. Do not add too much at once. If you finish using the stock and the rice still seems dry and uncooked, add boiling water by the ¼ cup. Total cooking time is approximately 30 minutes. Risotto should be tender but firm to the bite (al dente).

When the risotto is cooked, quickly and gently toss in the peppers, remaining tablespoon butter, cheese, salt, and pepper. Serve immediately.

RED PEPPER PASTA WITH ROASTED YELLOW PEPPERS

PREPARATION TIME: 30 MINUTES
SERVES: 8

1 medium red bell pepper, roasted
   and peeled* (see page 10)
6 medium yellow bell peppers, roasted
   and peeled (see page 10)
2 tablespoons olive oil
1 clove garlic, minced
1 tablespoon balsamic vinegar, or red
   wine vinegar with 1 teaspoon sugar
1 large egg
2¼ cups all-purpose flour
¼ teaspoon salt
4 quarts water
1-2 tablespoons olive oil
2 tablespoons freshly chopped parsley

Slice the peppers and devein and seed. Quarter the red pepper and set aside. Slice the yellow peppers into ¼-inch strips and place in a small saucepan. Add the oil, garlic, and vinegar. Set aside.

In a blender or food processor fitted with the steel blade, puree the red pepper for 5 seconds. Add the egg, *2 cups flour*, and salt and process 10 seconds more. Add the remaining flour by the tablespoon, processing until the dough leaves the side of the work bowl but remains soft. Process the dough 40 seconds or until smooth. Remove the dough and wrap in plastic. Allow to rest at room temperature 30 minutes.

Cut dough into eight pieces on a well-floured surface. Remove one of the eight pieces and cover the remaining pieces with plastic to prevent drying. With a pasta machine or by hand, roll and stretch each piece into a rectangular shape about 1/16 inch thick, sprinkling with the flour as necessary. Cut the pasta into desired shapes, using a pasta machine or by

(continued)

hand. Separate pasta strands and dry on paper towels or over a rack.

Bring the water to a rolling boil in a large pot. Add the fresh pasta and cook no more than 30 seconds. Drain. Toss with the 1–2 tablespoons olive oil and parsley.

Place the yellow peppers over low heat, stirring constantly. Arrange the pasta on a large platter or individual serving plates. Top with the yellow peppers. Garnish with the parsley.

*For a quicker version, substitute one 4-ounce jar pimientos for the red pepper.

PREPARATION TIME: 20 MINUTES
SERVES: 6 TO 8

8 ounces uncooked wide egg noodles
½ cup butter
1 *each* medium red and yellow bell
   pepper, deveined and seeded,
   chopped
½ cup heavy cream
1 cup freshly grated Parmesan cheese
Salt and freshly ground black pepper
   to taste
Dash of nutmeg
2 tablespoons freshly chopped parsley
Grated Parmesan cheese

Alfredo was a dashing Roman restaurateur known for his fine cuisine and high style. He tossed his noodles with a gold fork and spoon given to him by Mary Pickford and Douglas Fairbanks.

Cook the noodles according to the package directions and drain. In a large skillet, melt the butter over medium heat and sauté the peppers briefly until just soft, about 5 minutes. Stir in the cream, cheese, salt, pepper, and nutmeg. Pour the sauce over the hot noodles and toss until coated. Sprinkle with the parsley and pass the additional grated cheese.

SOUTH AMERICAN GREEN RICE

PREPARATION TIME: 1 HOUR
SERVES: 6

3 medium green bell peppers,
  deveined and seeded, chopped
4 Anaheim chiles, deveined and
  seeded, chopped
1 cup freshly chopped parsley
1 large onion, chopped
9 cloves garlic, chopped
2 teaspoons sugar
1 teaspoon dried oregano
½ teaspoon ground cumin
¼ cup vegetable oil
2 cups uncooked long grain white rice
5 cups chicken stock
¼ cup freshly chopped cilantro

Rice is a staple in a number of South American countries. In Argentina, the friends of one who has hit the skids will say, "Poor man, he's lost his rice."

In a blender or food processor fitted with the steel blade, puree the peppers, chiles, parsley, onion, garlic, sugar, oregano, and cumin.

In a large heavy skillet or casserole fitted with a tight lid, heat the oil until hot. Add the rice and stir to coat. Add the puree and simmer, stirring occasionally for 5 minutes. Add the stock and bring to a boil. Reduce the heat and simmer uncovered until the liquid is level with the rice, about 10 minutes. Cover and reduce heat to as low as possible. Cook 30 minutes. Turn off the heat and allow the rice to rest until tender. Toss in the cilantro and fluff with a fork.

FIERY FRIED RICE

PREPARATION TIME: 20 MINUTES
SERVES: 4

4 tablespoons peanut oil
1 egg lightly beaten with 1 tablespoon
water
1 medium onion, chopped
1 jalapeño pepper, deveined and
seeded, chopped
2 cloves garlic, minced
1 medium green bell pepper,
deveined and seeded, chopped
5 cups cooked long grain white rice
2 tablespoons raisins for garnish
3 scallions, chopped, for garnish

This is a recipe that originated in Singapore, Nasi Goreng. *It makes a spicy accompaniment to any simple dinner.*

In a wok or large skillet, heat *2 tablespoons peanut oil* and add the egg to the wok to make a thin omelette. Remove and allow to cool, then shred and reserve.

In a blender or food processor fitted with the steel blade, puree the onion, jalapeño, garlic, and bell pepper into a paste. Add the remaining oil to the wok and fry the paste gently, about 2 minutes. Gently toss in the rice, separating the grains and stir-frying as added. Toss and stir-fry 3 minutes. Top with shreds of egg, raisins, and scallions.

MEXICAN FRIED CHILES AND POTATOES

PREPARATION TIME: 30 MINUTES
SERVES: 6

2 pounds small red potatoes
8 Anaheim or poblano chiles, roasted
    and peeled (see page 10)
8 tablespoons vegetable oil
1 large onion, diced
Salt and freshly ground black pepper
    to taste

This makes a piquant accompaniment to roasted and broiled meats. The wonderful smell of fried chiles is a familiar call to lunch throughout Mexico.

In a large pot of boiling water, cook the potatoes about 10 minutes or until just tender. (Do not overcook.) Drain and dice, set aside.

Devein and seed the Anaheim chiles and cut into strips. In a large skillet, heat *6 tablespoons oil* and sauté the onion over medium heat until soft. Add the chile strips, cover, and cook over medium-low heat, about 8–10 minutes.

Remove the lid and add the remaining oil. Return the heat to medium and add the potatoes. Fry, stirring frequently, until golden brown, about 15 minutes. Be careful to keep stirring and turning to keep the chiles and onion from sticking to the bottom of the skillet. Serve immediately.

TROPICAL FRUIT CURRY

PREPARATION TIME: 1 HOUR 15 MINUTES
SERVES: 4

4 tablespoons unsalted butter
2 medium onions, thinly sliced
1 jalapeño pepper, deveined and
   seeded, chopped
1 medium red bell pepper, deveined
   and seeded, chopped
2 tablespoons curry powder
¼ cup pineapple pieces
½ cup chopped papaya*
2 bananas, peeled and cut into
   thick slices
1 medium green apple, cored and cut
   into pieces
2 tablespoons fresh lime juice
1 tablespoon lime zest
1½ cups unsweetened coconut milk**
½ cup unsweetened shredded coconut
½ teaspoon ground ginger
½ cup raisins
Steamed white rice
Fresh mint for garnish

Serve with Sri Lanka Curry *(see page 62) or as a companion to roast game hen or chicken.*

In a heavy saucepan, heat the butter and sauté the onions, jalapeño, and bell pepper until soft. Stir in the curry powder, then mix in the pineapple, papaya, banana, and apple pieces, lime juice and zest, and coconut milk. Cook 10 minutes, stirring occasionally. Stir in the coconut, ginger, and raisins until mixed well. Lower the heat and simmer 1 hour. Serve over the rice garnished with the mint.

*If papaya is not available, omit and increase the amount of pineapple.
**Unsweetened coconut milk is available at Indian specialty stores and in the ethnic section of most supermarkets.

MY MOTHER WORKED HER magic on everything she served. The grocery store coleslaw became confetti slaw with a handful of chopped red and green peppers. Canned tuna was transformed into a crunchy salad served in bright red "pepper boats." Any old green salad was perked up with a few slices of strategically placed pepper rings. Toss in peppers and suddenly, salads are something special.

The selections here are arranged from hearty main-course fare, to lighter tossed combinations, all with an eye for color and fancy.

YELLOW PEPPERS AND SHRIMP IN LEMON VINAIGRETTE

PREPARATION TIME: 10 MINUTES
SERVES: 4

1 pound cooked shrimp, peeled and
   deveined
2 medium yellow or orange bell
   peppers, deveined and seeded,
   chopped
2 scallions, chopped
Juice of 1 lemon
Zest of 1 lemon
Dash of cayenne powder
1 clove garlic, minced
Salt and freshly ground black pepper
   to taste
7 tablespoons olive oil
Lettuce leaves

This easy and pretty combination makes a refreshing first course or light main-course salad. It is offered as an appetizer on the menu at Cocolozone ("that Minneapolis Pasta Place"), but I often order it for lunch.

In a medium-size bowl, combine the shrimp, peppers, and scallions. In a small bowl, combine the lemon juice and zest, cayenne powder, garlic, salt, and pepper. Whisk in the olive oil in a slow, steady stream. Pour over the shrimp and peppers and toss to coat. Place the lettuce leaves on individual plates or a large serving platter. Arrange the shrimp and vegetables overall.

CRAB SALAD STUFFED PEPPERS

PREPARATION TIME: 15 MINUTES
SERVES: 2 TO 4

½ pound crab meat (fresh, frozen, or
    canned)
⅓ cup mayonnaise
3 scallions, chopped
1 medium red bell pepper, finely
    chopped
1 tablespoon freshly chopped tarragon
1 teaspoon finely grated lemon zest
2 tablespoons fresh lemon juice
Cayenne powder to taste
2 medium yellow, orange, or green
    bell peppers, deveined and seeded,
    cut in half horizontally
Lettuce leaves
Fresh tarragon for garnish

*This is my grown-up version of Mom's Tuna Boats. It still strikes
a fanciful chord in most adults.*

Drain the crab meat thoroughly and place in a medium-size
bowl. Add the mayonnaise, scallions, chopped red pepper,
tarragon, lemon zest, lemon juice, and cayenne powder.
Spoon the filling into the pepper halves. Line individual plates
with the lettuce leaves, place the stuffed peppers on the lettuce,
and garnish with the tarragon.

SALAD MARSEILLES

PREPARATION TIME: 15 MINUTES
SERVES: 2 TO 4

½ cup olive oil
1 white Holland pepper, deveined
and seeded, cut into strips
1 Anaheim chile, deveined and
seeded, cut into strips
1 Italian frying pepper, deveined and
seeded, cut into strips
1 *each* medium red and yellow bell
pepper, deveined and seeded,
cut into strips
4 cloves garlic, minced
1 medium tomato, coarsely chopped
Salt and freshly ground black pepper
to taste
4 hard-cooked eggs, peeled and
quartered
8 anchovy fillets
¼ cup freshly chopped dill

This salad, inspired by classic salads of the French Riviera, may be served as a first course for four or a main course for two.

In a large skillet set over medium heat, heat the oil and sauté the peppers and garlic until the peppers are wilted and just beginning to caramelize along the edges. Add the tomato and continue cooking until warmed through. Salt and pepper to taste. To serve, arrange the salad on individual plates or a large serving platter and garnish with the egg quarters and anchovies. Sprinkle with the dill. Best served warm or at room temperature.

MEXICAN CEVICHE

PREPARATION TIME: 15 MINUTES
MARINATING TIME: 1 HOUR
SERVES: 6

¾ cup fresh lime juice
1 teaspoon lime zest
3 tablespoons olive oil
1 medium purple onion, diced
2 medium tomatoes, diced
4 scallions, chopped
   (including green tops)
1 *each* medium red and yellow bell
   pepper, deveined and seeded,
   diced
1 jalapeño pepper, deveined and
   seeded, chopped

(continued)

This is actually a Peruvian method of "cooking" fish by marinating it in citrus juice, usually lime or lemon juice. The marinade preserves the texture and flavor of the fish without subjecting it to heat. It is critical that ceviche be made only with very fresh fish.

In a medium-size glass bowl, combine the first thirteen ingredients with the scallops and cover. Refrigerate at least 1 hour. Taste (you may want more chiles). To serve, remove the ceviche from the bowl with a slotted spoon and arrange on individual plates lined with the lettuce leaves. If desired, garnish with the cilantro and slices of lime.

VARIATIONS:
   ½ pound fresh shrimp, peeled and deveined
   ½ pound fresh sole, rinsed and cut into 1-inch pieces
   ½ pound fresh salmon, rinsed and cut into 1-inch pieces

3 cloves garlic, minced
4 tablespoons freshly chopped cilantro
¼ teaspoon ground cumin
½ teaspoon sugar
Salt and freshly ground black pepper
   to taste
½ pound fresh scallops, cut in
   half if large
Lettuce leaves
Fresh cilantro for garnish
Lime slices for garnish

GRILLED TURKEY BREAST
ON ROASTED GARLIC AND SWEET PEPPERS

PREPARATION TIME: 20 MINUTES
MARINATING TIME: 1 HOUR
SERVES: 6

4 turkey breast tenderloins
1½ cups olive oil
¼ cup chopped onions
2 tablespoons freshly chopped thyme
¼ cup fresh lemon juice
24 cloves garlic, peeled
3 *each* medium red and green bell
    peppers, deveined and seeded, cut
    into strips
1 tablespoon grated lemon peel
½ cup fresh lemon juice
2 teaspoons Dijon mustard
Lettuce leaves

Preheat the grill or broiler. Rinse and dry the turkey breasts and set in a nonaluminum pan. In a small bowl, combine ½ *cup oil*, onions, thyme, and the ¼ cup lemon juice, and pour the mixture over the turkey. Allow to marinate in the refrigerator at least 1 hour.

Remove the turkey and reserve the marinade. Grill over medium-low heat, basting frequently. Place the garlic cloves on a well-greased piece of aluminum foil and sprinkle with the remaining olive oil. Place the turkey and garlic on the grill and cover. Baste the turkey frequently, allowing 10 minutes per side. Stir the garlic occasionally. Turkey is done when the meat springs back and is no longer pink when cut. Remove the turkey and garlic from the grill and keep warm.

Thinly slice the garlic. In a large bowl, combine the garlic, peppers, and lemon peel. In a small bowl, whisk together the ½ cup lemon juice and mustard. Then whisk in the remaining oil in a slow, thin stream. Toss the mixture with the peppers. Line a large plate with the lettuce leaves and mound the peppers in the center . Cut the turkey into 1-inch pieces and pile on top of the peppers. Drizzle with the dressing remaining in the bowl.

TRICOLOR BELL PEPPERS AND ROAST BEEF SALAD
IN PESTO VINAIGRETTE

PREPARATION TIME: 20 MINUTES
SERVES: 6

1 *each* large red, yellow, and purple
   bell pepper, deveined and seeded,
   cut into strips
1 small sweet onion, thinly sliced
1 tablespoon Dijon mustard
⅓ cup red wine vinegar
1 cup freshly chopped basil leaves
1 cup olive oil
½ cup pine nuts
¾–1 pound roast beef, cut into
   thin strips
Salt and freshly ground black pepper
   to taste
1 medium head Boston lettuce,
   cut into leaves
Toasted pine nuts and fresh basil
   for garnish
Grated Parmesan cheese for garnish

In a medium-size bowl, combine the peppers and onion. In a blender or food processor fitted with the steel blade, process the mustard, vinegar, and basil, stopping to scrape down the sides of the bowl. While the motor is running, add the oil in a slow, steady stream, then the pine nuts all at once so they are coarsely chopped. Pour one-half of the dressing over the vegetables and toss. Add the beef and more dressing to coat well. (Extra vinaigrette will keep in the refrigerator 2–3 weeks and tastes great on any tossed salad.) Salt and pepper to taste. To serve, line a serving platter or individual plates with the lettuce leaves. Top with the salad and garnish with the pine nuts, basil, and cheese.

GRILLED PEPPER, SAUSAGE, AND POTATO SALAD

PREPARATION TIME: 30 MINUTES
SERVES: 4 TO 6

1½ pounds mild Italian sausages
2 pounds small red potatoes
1 *each* medium red, yellow, and
   green bell pepper, deveined and
   seeded, cut into strips
1 medium red onion, thinly sliced
3 tablespoons freshly chopped basil,
   or 4 teaspoons dried
¼ cup freshly chopped parsley
½ cup prepared vinaigrette
   salad dressing
Hard-cooked eggs and tomatoes,
   sliced for garnish
Fresh basil and parsley for garnish

This is an easy main dish or hearty side-dish salad. It's great to pack for picnics and barbecues. Because it is not made with mayonnaise, it will stand up to the summertime heat.

Prepare the grill for medium heat or preheat the broiler. Grill or broil the sausages 15–20 minutes until fully cooked. Let cool and slice diagonally into ½-inch pieces. Place in a large serving bowl.

In a large saucepan of boiling water, cook the potatoes until just tender, about 10 minutes. Drain, cook, and cut in half or quarters. Add to the sausages along with the peppers, onion, basil, and parsley.

In a large bowl, toss all the ingredients with the dressing. Serve garnished with slices of the egg and tomatoes, garnished with the basil and parsley.

PEPPER AND LEEK VINAIGRETTE

PREPARATION TIME: 15 MINUTES
MARINATING TIME: 1 HOUR
SERVES: 6

4 leeks, roots trimmed, cut into
    4 inches of green
1 medium red bell pepper, deveined
    and seeded, thinly sliced
3 tablespoons red wine vinegar
1 teaspoon Hungarian paprika
1 teaspoon Dijon mustard
½ teaspoon cayenne powder
¼ teaspoon sugar
3 teaspoons olive oil
Salt and freshly ground black pepper
    to taste

This light and spicy salad is classic Creole, combining the French influence (leeks with vinaigrette) with local ingredients (peppers and cayenne).

Split the leeks in half lengthwise. Rinse under cold running water. Bring a large pot of water to a full boil. Reduce the heat and cook until the leeks are tender, about 5 minutes. Drain and rinse with cold water to stop cooking. Toss with the pepper strips.

In a small bowl, combine the vinegar, paprika, mustard, cayenne powder, and sugar. Whisk in the olive oil, slowly. Add the salt and pepper. Pour over the leeks and pepper and toss. Cover and refrigerate 1 hour.

ROASTED BELL PEPPER AND ARUGULA SALAD

PREPARATION TIME: 20 MINUTES
SERVES: 6

2 bunches arugula*
1 small red onion, sliced
2 *each* medium red or yellow bell
   peppers, roasted and peeled (see
   page 10), deveined and seeded,
   thinly sliced
1 clove garlic, minced
1 teaspoon prepared mustard
3 tablespoons balsamic vinegar or red
   wine vinegar
1 cup olive oil
Salt and freshly ground black pepper
   to taste
1 medium head red or green leaf
   lettuce, cut into leaves

Arugula, also known as rocket or roquette, has a bright green serrated leaf with a spicy, mustardy tang. It is delicious paired with the sweet snap of fresh bell peppers.

Remove the arugula leaves from the stems, rinse, and thoroughly dry. Place in a medium-size bowl with the onion and peppers. In a small bowl, combine the garlic, mustard, and vinegar. Whisk in the olive oil. Salt and pepper to taste. Pour over the peppers and arugula and toss to coat. To serve, line a serving platter or individual plates with the lettuce leaves. Arrange the peppers and arugula on the leaves.

*2 cups watercress or escarole may be substituted for the arugula.

CONFETTI SLAW

PREPARATION TIME: 15 MINUTES
CHILLING TIME: 4 HOURS OR OVERNIGHT
SERVES: 6 TO 8

1 small head green cabbage,
   cleaned, cored, and shredded
1 *each* large red and green bell
   pepper, deveined and seeded,
   diced
1 cup mayonnaise
½ cup sour cream
2 tablespoons red wine vinegar
1 tablespoon Dijon mustard
2 teaspoons sugar
Salt and freshly ground black pepper
   to taste

This is the confetti version of deli-style coleslaw, made perky with peppery colors. It makes a great go-along for picnics, barbecues, and tailgate suppers.

In a large bowl, combine the cabbage and peppers. In a small bowl, whisk together the remaining ingredients. Pour the dressing over the vegetables and toss to combine. Cover and refrigerate at least 4 hours.

SUCCOTASH SALAD

PREPARATION TIME: 15 MINUTES
SERVES: 6

1 cup whole kernel corn
1 *each* medium red and green bell
   pepper, deveined and seeded,
   chopped
1 small red onion, finely chopped
4 scallions, chopped (including green
   tops)
1 cup cooked lima beans
¼ cup mayonnaise
¼ cup sour cream or sour half-and-
   half
1 tablespoon Dijon mustard
2 tablespoons red wine vinegar
2 teaspoons sugar
Salt and freshly ground black pepper
   to taste
Hungarian paprika for garnish

Succotash was a favorite of my grandmother's. The sweet pairing of summer corn and lima beans with ripe peppers made this cool salad a staple of our sweltering Jersey nights. She served this with fresh beefsteak tomatoes, a plate of cold meat, and plenty of iced tea in tall frosty glasses.

In a medium-size bowl, combine the vegetables. In a small bowl, whisk together the mayonnaise, sour cream, mustard, vinegar, sugar, salt, and pepper. Combine the dressing with the vegetables. Serve garnished with a dash of paprika.

MEXICAN TOSSED VEGETABLE SALAD

PREPARATION TIME: 15 MINUTES
SERVES: 6

2 Anaheim chiles, roasted and peeled
    (see page 10)
1 large very ripe avocado, peeled,
    pitted, and thinly sliced lengthwise
1 medium tomato, sliced
1 medium red bell pepper, deveined
    and seeded, sliced lengthwise
Lettuce leaves for garnish
Zest of 1 lime
Juice of 1 lime
2 tablespoons freshly chopped cilantro
⅛ teaspoon cayenne powder
1 clove garlic, minced
3 tablespoons olive oil
Salt and freshly ground black pepper
    to taste

According to Diane Kenney in THE CUISINES OF MEXICO, *years ago, salads were considered more appropriate fare for ladies than the meats offered to men because "they [women] are not as strong and lead a more sedentary life." An ensalada de damas (salad for ladies) might consist of cooked beets, green beans, peas, zucchini, and cauliflower tossed with pineapple, sweet potato, apples, avocado, olives, and pickled chiles. — from,* THE CUISINES OF MEXICO, *Diana Kennedy, Harper & Row, NYC, 1972, pg. 310.*

Devein and seed the Anaheim chiles and slice lengthwise. Arrange the chiles, avocado, tomato, and bell pepper over the lettuce leaves on a large serving platter or six individual serving plates. In a small bowl, whisk together the lime zest and juice, cilantro, cayenne powder, and garlic. Whisk in the olive oil. Salt and pepper to taste. Drizzle the dressing evenly over the salad.

MEXICAN JICAMA AND PEPPER SALAD

One 1-pound jicama
1 medium red bell pepper, deveined
    and seeded
1 tablespoon freshly chopped cilantro
1 small red onion, thinly sliced
Salt and freshly ground black pepper
    to taste
Zest of 1 orange
Sections of 1 orange with juice
Dash of chile powder for garnish

Jicama (pronounced "hik-a-ma"), sometimes called Mexican potato, is a large fat root grown in South America and Asia. It's known in China as a yam bean. Its thin brown skin is easy to peel using a sharp knife or potato peeler. Its flesh is juicy and crisp and almost sweet. In Mexico, it is often eaten as a snack — first marinated in lime juice, then sprinkled with chile powder.

Peel the brown skin of the jicama with a sharp knife or potato peeler and cut the jicama into thin strips. Cut the bell pepper into strips. In a medium-size bowl, combine the jicama, bell pepper, cilantro, onion, salt, and pepper. Toss with the orange zest and orange sections. Arrange on individual serving plates and sprinkle with the chile powder.

MINTED BROWN RICE AND BELL PEPPER SALAD

PREPARATION TIME: 1 HOUR
SERVES: 6

1 cup chicken stock
½ cup uncooked brown rice
½ cup finely chopped red onion
1 medium red, yellow, or green bell
    pepper, deveined and seeded,
    chopped
¼ cup fresh mint leaves
¼ cup fresh parsley
1 clove garlic
¼ cup olive oil
2 tablespoons white wine vinegar
Salt and freshly ground black pepper
    to taste
¼ cup toasted sunflower seeds

This is a variation of tabouli, a Syrian dish traditionally made with bulgur.

In a small saucepan, bring the chicken stock to a boil and add the brown rice. Reduce the heat, cover, and simmer until the liquid is absorbed, about 40 minutes. Turn into a large bowl and stir in the onion and pepper.

In a blender or food processor fitted with the steel blade, mince the mint, parsley, and garlic. While the machine is running, slowly add the oil and vinegar and process until well mixed. Pour the dressing over the rice and toss. Season with the salt and pepper. Refrigerate to cool. To serve, garnish with the sunflower seeds.

IT'S HARD TO KNOW how many pickled peppers Peter Piper picked. Two pecks of sweet cherry peppers, one of hot jalapeños? Was he picking for relish. Or maybe, his peppers became salsas, marmalades, jellies, butters, chutney, or barbecue sauce. Here's a peck of ideas and recipes for your pantry or pretty presents for you to pick.

RED HOT SALSA CRUDA

PREPARATION TIME: 15 MINUTES
MAKES: 3 CUPS

6 medium tomatoes, chopped
6 serrano or jalapeño chiles, or to taste,
    deveined and seeded, chopped
5 cloves garlic, minced
1 medium onion, chopped
5 scallions, chopped (including
    green tops)
½ cup freshly chopped cilantro
1 teaspoon sugar
Salt and freshly ground black pepper
    to taste

This fresh salsa is a Mexican classic, served throughout the country in cut-glass bowls set into cracked ice at fancy restaurants — in paper cups at truck stops. It's spicy and light and terrific with tortillas, guacamole, and chips, on scrambled eggs, macaroni and cheese, or grilled burgers — just about anything that needs color and spice.

In a blender or food processor fitted with the steel blade, process the tomatoes, chiles, and garlic until coarsely chopped. Turn into a medium-size bowl and add the remaining ingredients. Chill before serving.

GREEN SALSA

PREPARATION TIME: 10 MINUTES
MAKES: 1 CUP

2 cloves garlic, diced
½ cup freshly chopped cilantro
½ cup freshly chopped parsley
1 Anaheim chile, deveined and
    seeded, chopped
1 medium green bell pepper, deveined
    and seeded, chopped
Zest of 1 lime
Juice of 1 lime
½ cup olive oil
Salt and freshly ground black pepper
    to taste

Green Salsa (Salsa Verde) is a fresh, delicate sauce delicious with grilled vegetables, hard-cooked eggs, fresh crusty bread, or mild cheese.

   In a small bowl, combine all the ingredients thoroughly. Store in the refrigerator and use in two or three days.

HAITIAN HOT SAUCE

PREPARATION TIME: 10 MINUTES
MARINATING TIME: 1 HOUR
MAKES: 1 CUP

2 large onions, minced
2 cloves garlic, minced
6 tablespoons fresh lime juice
2 shallots, minced
2 serrano or jalapeño chiles, deveined
    and seeded, minced
3 tablespoons olive oil

Haitan Hot Sauce (Sauce Ti-Malice) is served with grilled meats and the classic Groits de Porc as well as a variety of other dishes. According to folklore, Bouki and Ti-Malice were two friends who loved grilled meat. Ti-Malice (the crafty one) prepared his grilled meat everyday for lunch. Bouki (the trusting) visited Ti-Malice at that time to chat and, of course, share the meat. In an attempt to break Bouki of his lunchtime visits, Ti-Malice prepared a fiery hot sauce and poured it over his meat one day. Bouki, however, delighted in the taste and ran through the street calling, "My friends, come and taste Ti-Malice sauce."

In a small saucepan, combine all the ingredients and bring to a boil over medium heat, stirring occasionally. Remove from the heat. Allow to cool. Refrigerate at least 1 hour before serving.

HOT AND SPICY BARBECUE SAUCE

PREPARATION TIME: 10 MINUTES
MAKES: 2½ CUPS

1 cup beer
Salt and freshly ground black pepper
    to taste
1 cup ketchup
4 tablespoons Worcestershire sauce
1 tablespoon Hungarian paprika
1 teaspoon crushed red hot chile
1 jalapeño pepper, deveined and
    seeded, minced
1 tablespoon Dijon mustard
1 tablespoon fresh lemon juice
1 medium onion, minced

Although the concept of cooking meat over an open fire goes back to the earliest days, the term barbecue comes from the Haitian word "barbacoca" meaning "framework of sticks." This referred to the grill-like structure made originally of sticks on which the meat was roasted. In the United States, barbecuing became a very popular means of social entertaining in Texas in the mid-1800s. An elaborate menu might include six cattle, twenty hogs, fifty sheep, pigs, lambs — and a wide variety of baked goods, especially corn breads.

Place all the ingredients in a medium-size saucepan and bring to a boil over medium heat. Lower the heat and simmer sauce 7–8 minutes, stirring occasionally. Delicious on ribs, chicken, turkey, and steak.

DRIED CHILE PASTE

PREPARATION TIME: 30 MINUTES
MAKES: ½ CUP

4–5 dried chiles (ancho, pasilla, or mulato), deveined and seeded
Boiling water
2–3 tablespoons vegetable oil

This piquant puree adds pizzaz to sauces, stews, soups, grilled cheese sandwiches, pizza, or crisp crackers and cream cheese.

Preheat oven to 350°F. Lightly toast the chiles in the oven 3–5 minutes, or until they've puffed up. Place in a small bowl and add just enough boiling water to cover. Let soak 20 minutes. Drain. Place in a blender or food processor fitted with the steel blade and puree with the oil to make a smooth paste. Store in a covered container in the refrigerator. This will keep several months.

CHILE BUTTER

PREPARATION TIME: 10 MINUTES
MAKES: ½ CUP

3 tablespoons *Dried Chile Paste* (see page 130)
½ cup softened unsalted butter
Zest of 1 lime
Juice of 1 lime
Fresh cilantro for garnish

This spicy pretty spread tastes great on fresh ears of corn, warm tortillas, or even plain bread sticks. Make double or triple the recipe and store in the freezer.

In a small bowl, work the paste together with the butter. Add the lime zest and lime juice. Turn into a small crock and garnish with the cilantro.

ROASTED RED PEPPER BUTTER

PREPARATION TIME: 20 MINUTES
MAKES: 1 CUP

1 clove garlic, pressed
¼ cup butter
1 medium red bell pepper, roasted
  and peeled (see page 10),
  deveined and seeded, chopped
Salt and freshly ground black pepper
  to taste

In a blender or food processor fitted with the steel blade, process the garlic with the butter. Add the pepper and puree until smooth. Transfer to a small dish and chill until hardened.

This delicious and pretty butter freezes nicely. Shape it into logs, wrap with aluminum foil, and freeze. Then serve it in ¼-inch slices on a decorative plate. It also makes a welcome gift.

SERVE *Roasted Red Pepper Butter*:
- on freshly cooked pasta.
- on grilled fish.
- spread on grilled cheese sandwiches.
- with fresh hot corn on the cob.
- with fresh hot corn bread.
- on baked potatoes.
- with hot popovers.

ROASTED PEPPER PESTO

PREPARATION TIME: 15 MINUTES
MAKES: 2 CUPS

2 *each* medium red and yellow bell
  peppers, roasted and peeled (see
  page 10), deveined and seeded
2 cloves garlic
2 cups packed fresh basil leaves
¼ cup olive oil

This makes a quick and easy sauce for pasta, a delicious spread for toasted French bread, a fragrant topping to ordinary grilled sausage or hamburgers, and a special addition to frozen pizza.

Slice the prepared peppers into thin strips, about ¼ inch, and place in a medium-size bowl. In a blender or food processor fitted with the steel blade, puree the garlic and basil leaves with the oil. Pour over the peppers. Toss, cover, and store in the refrigerator. This will taste even better the next day.

PEPPER WINE

PREPARATION TIME: 5 MINUTES
MAKES: 1½ CUPS

2 hot cherry peppers
1¼ cups dry sherry

Use Pepper Wine to add zest to stew (beef stew, goulash), soups (cream of mushroom, cheddar cheese), and sauces (cheese sauce, butter sauce). In Barbados, it is used to add a light peppery taste to sauces for meats that are sautéed or grilled. If you can't get hot cherry peppers, substitute serrano or jalapeño peppers.

Place the peppers in a sterilized jar. Add the sherry. Cover the jar and place in a dark area. Allow to stand several days.

CHILE PEPPER VINEGAR

PREPARATION TIME: 15 MINUTES
MARINATING TIME: 2 WEEKS
MAKES: 4 PINTS

8 cups cider vinegar
¼ cup sugar
14 serrano or jalapeño chiles,
   deveined and seeded, chopped
1 tablespoon peppercorns

This snappy vinegar adds bite to any poultry or meat marinade calling for vinegar, especially in Thai, Chinese, and Indian recipes. Try mixing a little into your favorite homemade or prepared Italian or vinaigrette dressing. Stir a little into a favorite prepared barbecue or sweet and sour barbecue sauce for tang.

In a large saucepan, combine all the ingredients and bring to a boil over medium heat, stirring constantly. Remove from the heat and cool to room temperature. Pour the mixture into a sterile 1-gallon jug. Cover and allow to stand two weeks in a cool dark place. Strain through cheesecloth into sterilized bottles. Store in a cool dark place. Will keep up to four months.

HOT PEPPER OIL

PREPARATION TIME: 5 MINUTES
MAKES: 1 CUP

¼ cup hot red pepper flakes or
   crushed hot peppers
1 cup vegetable oil

This is a fiery oil used in traditional Southeast Asian hot dishes. Try it in dipping sauces for egg rolls, in a stir-fry that needs a bit of fire, or drizzle it over a dish (with caution) just before serving. Hot chile peppers are not only good for food, but also for beauty — a recent book on beauty published in the French West Indies suggests using five red hot chile peppers macerated in 2 cups of oil to make hair thick and shiny.

In a small saucepan set over medium heat, bring the pepper flakes and oil to a boil. Turn off the heat and allow to cool. Strain into a glass container and seal. Store in the refrigerator.

OLD-FASHIONED PEPPER RELISH

PREPARATION TIME: 40 MINUTES
MAKES: 3 PINTS

½ cup mustard seed
1 pound green bell peppers, deveined
   and seeded, chopped
2 pounds red bell peppers, deveined
   and seeded, chopped
8 cups sugar
2 quarts white vinegar

This is the recipe my grandmother used to "put up" those beautiful fresh peppers for the winter. It tastes great on hot dogs and hamburgers or mixed into a little mayonnaise with horseradish sauce for fish.

Place all the ingredients in a large aluminum kettle and slowly bring to a boil, stirring until the sugar has dissolved. Boil 15–20 minutes, stirring frequently until liquid thickens. Pack into hot sterilized jars. Cover and process according to manufacturer's directions.

BELL PEPPER AND ONION MARMALADE

PREPARATION TIME: 1 HOUR
MAKES: 1 CUP

¼ cup olive oil
3 large onions, sliced
4 medium red bell peppers, deveined
   and seeded, sliced
1 medium green bell pepper,
   deveined and seeded, sliced
Salt and freshly ground black pepper
   to taste
2 tablespoons freshly chopped
   oregano, or 2 teaspoons dried
3 tablespoons freshly chopped basil,
   or 3 teaspoons dried
¼ cup freshly chopped parsley
½ - 1 cup chicken stock

This makes a wonderful appetizer served with crusty bread or crisp whole wheat crackers. Offer as a condiment to grilled chicken, pork, or steak. It also makes an unusually tasty sandwich spread for turkey, chicken, roast beef, ham and cheese, egg salad, and cream cheese sandwiches.

Heat the oil in a large skillet and sauté the onions and peppers over medium heat until the vegetables begin to soften, about 4 minutes. Lower the heat, add the salt, pepper, and herbs. Cook, uncovered, stirring occasionally, about 20 minutes. Vegetables should be very soft.

Add *½ cup stock* to moisten and cook another 15 minutes. As the mixture cooks down, add more stock by ¼ cupsful if necessary. The mixture should be thick and somewhat glossy, like marmalade. Serve warm or at room temperature. Store, covered, in the refrigerator.

PICKLED CHILE PEPPERS

PREPARATION TIME: 10 MINUTES
MARINATING TIME: 2 WEEKS
MAKES: 1 PINT

6 serrano or jalapeño chiles
3 cloves garlic, peeled
⅓ cup vegetable oil
2 sprigs fresh dill
1 teaspoon sugar
White wine vinegar

These Cajun pickled chiles are hot stuff. Cut them up and toss on burritos and tacos, add pizzaz to pizza, or chop and add to red beans and rice.

Make a slit in the side of each chile. Remove the veins and seeds but leave the chile whole. Fill a sterilized pint jar with the chiles. Add the garlic, oil, dill, and sugar. Fill the jar with the vinegar. Cover the jar and shake. Set in a cool place for at least two weeks. Once opened, store in the refrigerator.

PICKLED SWEET PEPPERS

PREPARATION TIME: 30 MINUTES
MARINATING TIME: 2 WEEKS
MAKES: 8 PINTS

3 pounds sweet cherry peppers,
    whole, or 3 pounds red and yellow
    bell peppers, deveined and seeded,
    cut into large squares
3 cups white wine vinegar
3 cups water
4 tablespoons salt
2 tablespoons sugar

These pretty peppers make a great gift for a favorite gourmet. They are colorful accompaniments to grilled turkey breast, cold sliced roast beef or ham, fried chicken, or roast pork. Thanks Peter Piper.

Pack the peppers into clean sterilized jars. In a large saucepan, combine the vinegar, water, salt, and sugar and bring to a boil over high heat, stirring frequently. Remove from the heat and pour the mixture into the jars, filling ½ inch from the rim. Seal the jars and process according to manufacturer's directions. Allow peppers to stand two weeks before using.

FIERY INDIAN CHUTNEY

PREPARATION TIME: 45 MINUTES
MARINATING TIME: 6 MONTHS
MAKES: 1 QUART

7 tart apples, cored and cut into cubes
1 medium onion, chopped
10 cloves garlic
1 jalapeño pepper, deveined and
    seeded, chopped
1 cup raisins
1⅓ cups packed brown sugar
2 cups cider vinegar
2 tablespoons mustard seed
¼ cup ground ginger

This is a hot and fiery chutney, so use with care. Serve with Sri Lanka Curry *(see page 62), on top of cream cheese with crackers, or as a side dish to roast pork.*

Place the apples, onion, and garlic in a large saucepan and add enough water just to cover. Simmer over low heat until soft, about 10 minutes. Add the remaining ingredients. Bring to a boil, reduce the heat, and simmer 15–20 minutes until the mixture is thick. Pack into clean sterilized jars. Cover and process the jars according to manufacturer's directions. Store in a cool dark place six months to allow spices and flavors to marry before using.

JALAPEÑO JELLY

PREPARATION TIME: 30 MINUTES
MAKES: 4 PINTS

8 jalapeño peppers, deveined
  and seeded
8 medium green bell peppers,
  deveined and seeded
2 cups white wine vinegar
10 cups sugar
2 bottles liquid pectin

This makes a great gift. Serve with roast or grilled leg of lamb in lieu of mint jelly. Spread on sandwiches of spicy ham and tomato. Melt in a small saucepan and use to glaze grilled chicken or game hens. Serve with grilled or roast pork or chicken. (I've been caught spreading it on crackers with peanut butter or spooning it up straight from the jar.)

In a blender or food processor fitted with the steel blade, puree the peppers. Turn into a medium-size saucepan. Add the vinegar and bring to a boil. Reduce the heat and simmer 5 minutes. Cool, then strain juice through a strainer lined with two layers of cheesecloth. Squeeze to extract all the juices. Discard the solids. Add the sugar to the juice and bring to a boil. Reduce the heat and simmer 10 minutes. Add the pectin and boil 1 minute. Pour into clean sterilized jars and process according to manufacturer's directions. Store in a cool dry place. Once opened, store the jelly in the refrigerator.

AT TEJAS, A SOUTHWESTERN cafe in downtown Minneapolis, blue cornmeal hot pepper corn sticks served with plenty of sweet cream butter are my answer to the midwinter blahs. Baked in old-fashioned cast-iron molds, they are light and moist with a toasty crust. My sister and I have been known to make an entire dinner of them with a small green salad and plenty of beer.

Try adding chopped red, green, and yellow bell pepper to your favorite corn bread mix or herb bread recipe for color and flavor, or a little hot chile (1 fresh jalapeño per loaf) for zest. Serve with a crock of *Chile Butter*, *Roasted Red Pepper Butter*, or *Bell Pepper and Onion Marmalade* (see chapter on Condiments).

CORNY RED PEPPER CORN BREAD

PREPARATION TIME: 10 MINUTES
MAKES: ONE 8 BY 8-INCH PAN

1 small package corn muffin mix
1 small red bell pepper, deveined and
   seeded, chopped
½ cup whole kernel corn

Prepare the mix according to package directions. Add the bell pepper and corn and turn into a greased pan. Bake according to package directions.

VARIATION:
HOT PEPPER AND CHEESE CORN BREAD
Substitute 1 deveined, seeded, and chopped jalapeño pepper for the red bell pepper. Omit the corn. Add ½ cup shredded sharp cheddar cheese. Follow above directions.

JALAPEÑO AND RED PEPPER CORN STICKS

PREPARATION TIME: 15 MINUTES
BAKING TIME: 20 MINUTES
MAKES: 14 STICKS

Vegetable oil
1 cup blue cornmeal*
1 cup all-purpose flour
½ teaspoon salt
1 teaspoon sugar
1 tablespoon baking powder
2 eggs
1 cup milk
1 jalapeño pepper, deveined and
 seeded, chopped
1 medium red bell pepper, deveined
 and seeded, chopped
2 tablespoons melted butter

Using a cast-iron corn or muffin pan produces a delicious crunchy crust. The chile adds bite, while the sweet, mild bell pepper adds color.

Preheat oven to 425°F. Liberally grease a corn stick pan with the vegetable oil. In a large bowl, combine the cornmeal, flour, salt, sugar, and baking powder. In a small separate bowl, beat the eggs with the milk. Make a well in the dry ingredients and add the wet ingredients all at once. Stir just to combine, the batter will be lumpy. Gently fold in the peppers and butter. Fill the molds almost to the top with the batter and bake 20 minutes. Serve warm with lots of butter.

---

*Blue cornmeal is available in Mexican specialty stores and in the ethnic department of major supermarkets. Blue cornmeal originated in Santa Fe, New Mexico, where the dark exotic corn is a staple. Blue cornmeal is coarser, heavier, and nuttier tasting than yellow cornmeal. One may be substituted for the other quite easily.

ROASTED PEPPER AND CHEESE BREAD

PREPARATION TIME: 30 MINUTES
RISING TIME: 2 HOURS
BAKING TIME: 1 HOUR
MAKES: 2 LOAVES

1 *each* red and yellow bell pepper,
    roasted and peeled (see page 10),
    deveined and seeded
2 packages active dry yeast
1¼ cups warm water
1 teaspoon sugar
2 teaspoons salt
¼ teaspoon cayenne powder
1 teaspoon chile powder
1 teaspoon caraway seeds
½ cup lukewarm milk
1½ cups whole wheat flour
1 cup freshly grated cheddar cheese
3 cups all-purpose flour
1 tablespoon melted butter

This crusty, fragrant loaf is delicious with Sheilia's Pumpkin and Roasted Pepper Soup (see page 42), or Tricolor Bell Peppers and Roast Beef Salad (see page 116). Try serving it warmed with chèvre as an appetizer or slicing lengthwise for thick-grilled cheddar cheese and tomato sandwiches.

Dice the prepared peppers evenly and set aside. In a large bowl, dissolve the yeast in *¼ cup warm water*. Let stand, then stir in the sugar, salt, cayenne powder, chile powder, diced peppers, caraway seeds, and milk. Stir in the whole wheat flour alternately with the remaining water. Add the cheese.

Slowly beat in *2 cups all-purpose flour* using a wooden spoon. Turn the dough onto a lightly floured surface and knead for 15 minutes incorporating the remaining flour. When the dough is smooth and elastic, let stand 5 minutes.

Divide the dough in half. Roll each half into long Italian-style loaves and place in bread pans or on a baking sheet. Cover with a towel and allow to stand 1½–2 hours or until double in volume.

Slash the top of each loaf with a sharp knife and brush with the butter. Place a roasting pan, half-filled with water, in the bottom of the oven. Place the bread in the top half of the oven

(continued)

and bake 15 minutes. Reduce the heat to 325°F. and continue baking 35 minutes, or until the loaves are golden and sound hollow when tapped. Remove from the oven and cool on a wire rack.

TEXAS-STYLE SPOON BREAD

PREPARATION TIME: 10 MINUTES
BAKING TIME: 30 MINUTES
SERVES: 6

1 slice bacon, cut into 1-inch squares
¾ cup cornmeal
1 cup boiling water
2 tablespoons melted butter
2 tablespoons melted bacon fat
3 eggs, lightly beaten
2 teaspoons baking powder
1 cup buttermilk
1 tablespoon molasses
1 jalapeño pepper, deveined and
  seeded, chopped

The term "spoon bread" may have come from an Indian word for porridge, "suppawn," or from the fact that the dish is usually eaten with a spoon. Here is this southern classic with a Lone Star twist.

Preheat oven to 350°F. Place the bacon in a heavy ovenproof skillet or casserole and place in the oven. In a medium-size bowl, mix the cornmeal and boiling water and let steep 5 minutes. Add the butter and the bacon fat and mix well. Stir in the eggs, baking powder, buttermilk, and molasses. Add the jalapeño and stir. Pour the mixture over the bacon in the hot skillet. Return to the oven and bake 30 minutes. Serve with a spoon.

PREPARATION TIME: 20 MINUTES
RISING TIME: 40 MINUTES
BAKING TIME: 30 MINUTES
MAKES: ONE 10-INCH LOAF

2 packages active dry yeast
1 cup warm water
1 teaspoon salt
3 tablespoons olive oil
¼ teaspoon sugar
2½ cups all-purpose flour
2 teaspoons olive oil
1 *each* medium red and yellow bell
    pepper, deveined and seeded,
    chopped
1 tablespoon freshly chopped
    rosemary, or 1 teaspoon dried
¼ cup freshly grated Parmesan cheese

Foccaccia, an Italian olive oil bread, is a flat round bread, much like a pizza. The dough is tender and fragrant and easy to handle, requiring only one rising. For a toasty crust, bake this bread on a pizza stone.

In a large bowl, dissolve the yeast in the warm water. Add the salt, 3 tablespoons olive oil, and sugar. Slowly add the flour, stirring in ½ cup at a time. Turn the dough onto a lightly floured surface and knead it, adding only enough flour to prevent sticking. When the dough is smooth, shiny, and elastic, set in a lightly oiled bowl and rub with the 2 teaspoons olive oil. Cover with a towel, place in a warm area, and allow to rise about 40 minutes or until double in bulk.

Preheat oven to 450°F. Punch down and turn dough onto a hard surface. Shape into a 10-inch oval about ½ inch thick. Make cuts through the center of the oval. Transfer the loaf to an oiled baking sheet. In a small bowl, toss the peppers with the rosemary and spread over the bread. Press into the dough with the back of a spoon. Set aside to rise 20 minutes.

Place the baking sheet in the top half of the oven and bake 20 minutes. Remove and sprinkle with the cheese and return to the oven 10 minutes, or until the loaf is nicely browned and sounds hollow when tapped. Remove from the oven and cool on a wire rack.

SOUTH OF THE BORDER BISCUITS

PREPARATION TIME: 15 MINUTES
BAKING TIME: 15-20 MINUTES
MAKES: 24 BISCUITS

¼ pound cooked bacon, crumbled
1 jalapeño pepper, deveined and
     seeded, diced
1 medium red bell pepper, deveined
     and seeded, diced
4 scallions, chopped (including
     green tops)
1 cup freshly shredded cheddar
     cheese
3⅓ cups buttermilk biscuit mix
1 cup buttermilk
Flour

These savory biscuits are great with scrambled eggs and salsa.

Preheat oven to 350°F. Grease a large baking sheet. In a large bowl, combine the bacon, peppers, scallions, and cheese with the biscuit mix. Stir in the buttermilk until thoroughly combined to form a soft dough. Place the dough on a lightly floured surface and knead lightly. Roll the dough into ¾ – 1-inch thickness using a floured rolling pin. Cut the biscuits with a floured 2-inch cutter or a glass tumbler. Place in the oven and bake 15–20 minutes, or until the biscuits are light golden and sound hollow when tapped. Remove from the oven and cool on a wire rack.

CHEDDAR AND RED PEPPER MUFFINS

PREPARATION TIME: 10 MINUTES
BAKING TIME: 20 MINUTES
MAKES: 12 MUFFINS

2 eggs
¼ cup honey
¼ cup vegetable oil
½ cup buttermilk
1 cup freshly grated cheddar cheese
1 teaspoon Dijon mustard
1 medium red bell pepper, deveined
    and seeded, chopped
1¼ cups all-purpose flour
¼ cup whole wheat flour
½ teaspoon baking powder
½ teaspoon baking soda
½ teaspoon salt

These rich, savory muffins are great with Pepper and Cheddar Chowder, Corn and Chile Chowder, *and* Hot and Spicy Red Pepper and Cabbage Soup *(see chapter on Soups).*

Preheat oven to 400°F. Grease muffin tins or line with paper liners. In a large bowl, combine the eggs, honey, oil, buttermilk, cheese, mustard, and bell pepper. In a small bowl, sift together the all-purpose flour, whole wheat flour, baking powder, baking soda, and salt. Make a well in the dry ingredients and add the wet ingredients all at once. Stir to combine (batter will be lumpy). Turn into the muffin tins. Bake 20 minutes, or until a tester inserted in the center of a muffin comes out clean.

RED PEPPER, PEANUT BUTTER, AND BACON MUFFINS

PREPARATION TIME: 15 MINUTES
BAKING TIME: 20–25 MINUTES
MAKES: 12 LARGE OR 30 TINY MUFFINS

3 strips bacon
1 small red bell pepper, deveined and seeded, chopped
2 cups all-purpose flour
1 tablespoon baking powder
1 tablespoon brown sugar
½ teaspoon salt
1 egg, lightly beaten
1 cup milk
2 tablespoons melted bacon fat
Freshly ground black pepper to taste
4 tablespoons peanut butter

The Park Row Inn in St. Peter, Minnesota, is a quaint Victorian B & B where guests enjoy the generous hospitality of Ann Burckhardt, a food writer, cookbook author, and columnist for The Star Tribune. Guests have free range of the fragrant herb garden, access to Ann's rare cookbook collection as well as the bottomless homemade cookie jar. The Park Row Inn is renowned for its bountiful breakfasts — both country style with the works and heart healthy for guiltless indulgence. Muffins and homebaked breads are Ann's signatures. This unique creation is offered on occasion, a real conversation piece, as well as sumptuous Apple Pecan, Sour Cream, and Oat Bran muffin originals.

Preheat oven to 400°F. In a medium-size skillet, cook the bacon with the bell pepper until the bacon is crisp and the pepper is soft. Reserve the bacon fat. Drain the bacon on paper towels, then crumble and set aside. Grease the muffin tins or line with paper liners. In a large bowl, combine the flour, baking powder, brown sugar, and salt. In a small bowl, beat together the egg, milk, bacon fat, crumbled bacon, and pepper. Make a well in the flour mixture. Add the liquid

(continued)

mixture all at once and stir just until combined. Pour some batter into each muffin cup, then drop about ½ teaspoon of peanut butter into each cup and continue filling muffin cups until ¾ full. (If you're using the tiny muffin cups, you'll need far less peanut butter.) Bake 20–25 minutes (less for tiny muffins), or until a tester inserted in the center of a muffin comes out clean.